PRAISE FOR *SUCCESS FRAMES*

If you think learning from your failures is the fastest path to success, think again. Rob Hatch has a better plan: ask yourself, "What has worked for me in the past?" *Success Frames* lays out an easy-to-implement concept that sets aside what went wrong and instead focuses on what went right. All you have to do is follow it!

Kate Erickson Dumas, COO at Entrepreneurs on Fire

If you've ever heard that "success leaves clues" but couldn't figure out how to find and apply those clues, this book is for you. Rob Hatch demystifies the process so you can create frameworks that help you achieve your definition of success.

Dr. Michelle Mazur, author of the *3 Word Rebellion*

I've always been a firm believer in playing to my strengths to move things forward when life gets tough, and Rob's methodology of success frameworks has given me a process to follow which increases the value I get from this approach. So many coaches want to "fix" what's broken. Rob's use of core strengths to build confidence and reposition one's perspective is so much more energizing! The impacts last longer as learning to recognize your unique talents is such a necessary skill.

Mari Anne Snow, CEO, Co-Founder of Eascra Biotech

SUCCESS FRAMES

Why learning from **success** is the key to understanding what **motivates** and **inspires** us

ROB HATCH

First published in Great Britain by Practical Inspiration Publishing, 2024

ISBN   9781788604239   (print)
       9781788604253   (epub)
       9781788604246   (mobi)

Want to bulk-buy copies of this book for your team and colleagues? We can customize the content and co-brand *Success Frames* to suit your business's needs.

Please email info@practicalinspiration.com for more details.

 Practical Inspiration
Publishing

CONTENTS

ACKNOWLEDGMENTS

To my children, Aidan, Clay, Lucy, and Sitota, and my wife, Megin. You are the only success that matters.

PART I

THE MYTHS OF FAILURE

CHAPTER 1

THE POWER OF YOUR PAST SUCCESS—WHY FAILURE IS FAILING US

When I ask people how they did something successfully, it's often met with an uncomfortable silence, shrugging off the question. A few may sheepishly mutter comments such as, "I don't know, I just did it," or "I work hard." However, if I ask that same person why they failed, the list of reasons suddenly rolls off the tongue.

We've all heard quotes about learning from our mistakes. Time and again we've been told that failure is the best teacher. So pervasive is this idea that it's embraced and restated by the likes of Henry Ford and Bill Gates and accepted as virtual gospel by anyone aspiring to achieve almost anything.

Here are a few choice quotes from arguably some of the most successful people in the world.

"Failure is success if we learn from it."
—Malcolm Forbes

"It's fine to celebrate success but it is more important to heed the lessons of failure."
—Bill Gates

"We learn from failure, not from success!"
—Bram Stoker

There are dozens more from some of the most successful and prominent figures in history, all pointing to failure as the ultimate teacher. They clearly have a unique insight into what it takes to achieve the heights of success to which others have only dreamed.

How could we possibly argue?

But what if this well-worn notion that "failure is the best teacher" is nothing more than a romanticized version of the story. What if it's revisionist history? New research suggests that we learn more from our successes than our failures.

The hard truth of it all is that we fail miserably at learning from our failures. As adults, we're far beyond the simplicity of childhood experiences such as: "Touches hot stove. Burns hand. Knows not to touch hot stove."

Failure doesn't always reveal itself in a clear and tangible way. Yet we tend to approach our mistakes as though we've reached a dead end in life's maze. We've convinced ourselves that our brain holds a catalog of our attempts and variations and that it knows precisely what we need to avoid next time.

We can't simply shrug our shoulders and say, "Well, that didn't work. Let me try again this way." You and I both know that's not how this works. There's a big difference between knowing something didn't work and identifying what went wrong, when it occurred, and how to adjust your approach. Particularly when it comes to working with other people.

For one, communications are far more complex. Our interactions with others are nuanced. The more people we're working with compounds the issue. And the problems we're trying to solve often require a variety of approaches. There are many opportunities for things to go wrong, which makes it harder to isolate the failure and know exactly what it was and how to fix it.

How will you know?

Larger organizations have established protocols and resources for detecting when a failure occurs. Often before something small becomes catastrophic. They have teams that can analyze the mistake and implement new procedures.

It's worth noting that many of these mistakes come from not following the model of success that was laid out in the first place.

Our own methods of detection aren't as well trained or consistently implemented. Our ability to analyze and adjust is limited as well.

Failure is a bad teacher

There will be mistakes and missteps in the journey to becoming successful. We all have bad days. We all make mistakes. Failing is a part of the process of virtually *any* achievement. However, our failures aren't as instructive as we've come to accept.

Ayelet Fishbach is a researcher and faculty member at the prestigious Chicago Booth University Business School. She's renowned for her expertise and research in the areas of motivation and decision-making. Fishbach and postdoctoral fellow Lauren Eskreis-Winkler decided to put the theory of failure as the best teacher to the test. They conducted a series of five experiments, variations of a test, wherein participants were split into groups and asked a series of questions with two possible answers. The test was designed such that it didn't rely on the participant's knowledge, rather each person was essentially making a best guess at the correct answer.

An example of the type of question they asked might be, "Which is the more popular color among teenagers, purple or yellow?" Note that this wasn't taken from the test itself. However, this question doesn't rely on a specific set of knowledge, and there's only one correct answer. As you might expect, some got it right and others got it wrong.

The two groups of participants were then given feedback on the results of the test. One group was given *failure feedback* and shown the answers they got wrong. The other group was given *success feedback* and shown the answers they got right. Given that there were only two possible answers to each question, the "correct" answer was evident *regardless* of whether participants were given feedback on their failures or their successes.

Participants were then retested on the same set of questions. Again, every participant had access to the correct answer either by getting it correct the first time (the success feedback), or through their previous mistake (the failure feedback), as there were only two options for each question. However, in the retest, participants who were given failure feedback showed no improvement on the retest.

They were able to replicate their previous correct choices, but even though their mistakes were clearly pointed out, they failed to learn from them. And remember, the correct answer was obvious, regardless of the type of feedback participants received.

Fishbach and Eskreis-Winkler replicated the process to try to understand the reasons. In addition to created variations of the experiment, they surveyed participants from each group regarding their level of self-esteem after receiving feedback. The results showed that the failure feedback group reported lower self-esteem. Another term for this is "ego-threat." In other words, receiving feedback about what they did wrong was perceived as a threat.

To further confirm the existence of "ego-threat" and its negative impact, another variation of the test was given. In this instance, participants were given feedback on the mistakes someone *else* made, thus making it less personal. This was the only instance in which failure proved somewhat useful as a tool for learning. Learning from the mistakes of others proved to be more instructive than making the mistake themselves.

Fear and failure

The relationship between fear and failure is clearly very strong. However, it's not enough to say we're afraid of failing. That's oversimplifying the powerful psychological and neurological forces at work.

The participants in this study clearly failed, and not only those who were in the "failure feedback" group. *All* of them failed at some of the questions. The key difference was in the type of feedback they received.

What Fishbach's study reveals is critical to understanding why failure may not be the source of knowledge we've celebrated it to be: *Our ego gets in the way.* We're fragile and arrogant creatures. How then can we learn from something we're not keen to examine in the first place?

Likewise, since failure is such a threat to our ego, it keeps us from even looking at it. What experiences or examples show us *how* to learn from it? We don't have a model or blueprint for extracting lessons from failure.

So, despite what we've been led to believe, our failures aren't the rich well of instruction we've held them up to be. At best, they taught us what *not* to do. At worst, they're the third rail of our individual mental models, embarrassing enough that we essentially wince and recoil when they're pointed out to us.

Failure is failing us

A friend shared a recent experience when, after a call with a potential client, they sensed it didn't go well. It's happened to all of us. But what happens *next*?

After the call, they reflected on *why* it didn't go well, and realized they weren't as clear as they could have been. They also didn't establish the next steps with the client. My friend reassured themself they would do better next time, but I wasn't convinced, and neither were they.

You might be thinking, "Isn't that an example of learning from failure?" Not quite. And here's where failing... well, failed them.

1. Their reflection didn't reveal something new.

By reviewing the interaction, they did identify a gap in their process in *this* instance. For whatever reason, they missed a key step, something they've done many times to close a deal successfully. They already have a proven framework for closing a sale. They simply didn't apply it in this situation.

Their failure to follow through wasn't instructive. It only pointed out an instance of forgetfulness or a lack of consistency in their approach.

2. They don't have a plan to integrate what they identified in their reflection.

My friend also confessed they don't have a process to take those reflections and learn from them. It was just an acknowledgment that they forgot and that they would keep it in mind for the next time.

We all *think* we'll remember. And sometimes we do. But this belief that we learn from failure has many of us convinced it's an automatic process and we'll do better next time. "Next time I'll be sure to..."

You might have said something like this to yourself. But we all know it doesn't necessarily work that way. We get busy. We forget. And we're *all* guilty of making the same mistakes again.

The fact that this person took a moment to reflect on what went wrong is impressive all by itself. We don't typically put in the work to learn from what went wrong. And, as Fishbach's study alludes, we're reticent to think about it.

Don't take that too personally. It's hard work, and we may have never been taught how to do this. We've accepted the widely held belief that experience does it for us, naturally. But it takes much more than that.

Start with what works

> "Adults don't learn from doing. They learn by reflecting on what they have done."
> —John Dewey

I like to start with success. I know. Wouldn't we all?

In the process of reflecting on what we've done, we tend to focus on what went *wrong*, to zoom in too closely on our flaws and our deficits. It's always with the best of intentions, of course. We believe that if we could just eliminate *that* mistake, the rest will take care of itself.

The same is true when we focus on our weaknesses, on eliminating them, or at least shoring them up. We think, if I could just build this aspect of myself up, things will go more smoothly. While there may be *a kernel* of truth to this, one of the best ways to buttress our weaknesses is to first understand and utilize our strengths.

When building the framework for a house, we don't work from a plan developed showing us what *not* to do. No, it's drafted based on what we know will support the structure of the building. There are *core principles* for building a strong foundation and framework.

To replicate the core principles of building a successful structure, we need to understand *what it looks like* when things go right.

Since my friend has had successful calls with potential clients in the past. They already know what success looks like. That's where it starts.

Reflecting on what worked

If I were coaching this person, I would begin with what has worked for them before. So, I might ask…

- In the past, when you've landed your ideal clients, what did you do?
- What are all the steps leading up to setting the meeting?
- Did you prepare for the meeting? How?
- What do you typically have with you on hand as you begin the conversation?
- What happens during the meeting?
- How do you end your meetings with potential clients?
- What happens after the meeting?

We could add more, but *this* is how we would start to identify a simple framework for how to close a sale based on their prior success. The goal is to establish a process they can replicate, rooted in what they've already done. More specifically, grounded in what worked for them.

Success forms the foundation for any framework you'll construct. In this example, the questions I'm asking point to some common elements of success in most endeavors that are potential elements of her framework. Here are three:

- Preparation
- Structure of meeting
- Follow-up

The development of *her* framework will involve a bit more detail explaining what *preparation* looks like for her. All of this is designed to build out a framework that's anchored in her own successful experiences.

As such, it will suit her personal style and reflect her strengths with evidence that it has worked in the past.

Establishing a simple "Success Frame" is also helpful for evaluating each effort. Should she experience failure, it can help pinpoint where, when, and how things went wrong. Maybe a skipped step, such as "failing to establish next steps." But again, in this case, her *failure* was the result of not executing her complete framework for success.

If that's the case, what's the lesson she should extract? It seems like the lesson is simply... *follow the steps that you know lead to success.* Of course, that's what her prior success taught her.

Failing isn't a magical path to success. It either points out a gap in our execution or a gap in our knowledge. And our pursuit of knowledge to fill *that* gap often involves learning from someone *else* what success looks like, their *success frame.*

"Be Like Mike"

We crave success. We revere it. We admire it. We seek it out. We want to mimic it. Well, the success mostly, but not always the work.

The way we elevate the status of successful athletes provides the clearest evidence. One of Gatorade's most successful marketing campaigns featured Michael Jordan in their "Be Like Mike" ads. Michael Jordan is arguably the greatest basketball player of all time. The campaign leveraged the desires of an entire generation of future basketball players hoping to emulate his moves, his style, and most notably, his ability to seemingly take flight.

You'll notice they didn't go with, "Fail Like Mike." I mean, it may have been in contention. I wasn't in the room at the time so I can't be sure. Gatorade encouraged you to emulate him, at least insofar as it meant drinking their product.

One person who took this to heart was another National Basketball Association (NBA) legend, Kobe Bryant. Kobe modeled his entire game after Michael Jordan and ended up becoming an icon in his own right. A few minutes on YouTube will deliver side-by-side comparisons of the two. The resemblance in their physical movement is uncanny, right down to the way they stick out their tongue.

Kobe Bryant would be in *any* discussion of the top five best basketball players of all time. One of the unique things *he* was known for was his "Mamba Mentality," which can be roughly characterized by an *unrelenting drive to be the best.*

Quotes from Kobe about his winning mindset adorn basketball courts all over the world, encouraging players to adopt this same "Mamba Mentality." What those quotes splashed across gym walls and on posters in the bedrooms of aspiring basketball stars clearly don't say is, "Adopt a failure mentality."

In our pursuit of success, no matter how significant, whether it be a diet, a fitness goal, or some other lifestyle change, whether it's to rise to the level of athletic prowess to redefine a game, or contribute to redefining an industry or genre, we look to the examples others have set for *success*. We want to know their secrets. We read articles and biographies desperate to understand how to replicate the *success* of those we admire.

Why then do we still elevate failure as the best teacher?

What about...?

You may already know the story about Michael Jordan when he was in high school. If you do, it may have popped into your head as you read this.

The story goes that when Michael was in high school he *failed* to make the varsity basketball team. For years this story held an almost mythical status. It was elevated as the ultimate example of learning from failure. The way this story was *initially* told (and retold for decades) was that he was *cut* from his high school team.

What we were left with was an image of young Michael sent home, alone with only his thoughts and a desire to work hard and try again next year. However, he wasn't cut from his team. Due to his size and skillset at the time, he was (not unlike many basketball players) relegated to the junior varsity squad to further develop his skills. Sure, we can view it as *failing to make the varsity team*, but let's play this out...

Did that failure teach Michael something useful? According to Michael, it fueled his desire. In his words: "Whenever I was working out and got tired and figured I ought to stop, I would close my eyes and see that list in the locker room without my name on it. That usually got me going again."

Maybe that's enough. But is it enough to elevate failure to the status it has been given? I don't think it is. Let's say, though, that it taught him persistence in the face of a setback. That said, has there ever been a road to athletic achievement that didn't require persistence?

Maybe Michael hadn't learned this yet. And it *is* a valuable lesson to learn, but here's the thing: Michael used his failure to fuel his drive. He did indeed persist. But had he *continued* to fail, the lesson of hard work and persistence paying off may never have been learned. I mean, a *lot* of people work hard but never make it to varsity.

It stands to reason, then, that the lesson of hard work paying off can *only* become internalized when we achieve some level of success. In Michael's case, the first instance where hard work paid off was when he won his sixth NBA championship. One of his *first* accomplishments was simply making the varsity team.

This is critical to understanding how Success Frames develop and the reason why experiencing success and building upon it is so valuable.

Defining success

How do *you* define success?

In the world of sports, particularly for franchises with long-standing traditions of winning, it's hard to define it as anything *other* than winning a championship. This idea is so pervasive that if you were to interview elite athletes on the subject you may note a hint of reticence to even acknowledge that anything other than the ultimate prize could be viewed as successful.

However, even when a team fails to reach that level of success, or when they fail to reach a level of even *contending* for the opportunity to win a championship, those same players will strike a different tone when it comes to contract negotiations and their worth.

Imagine a player walking into a contract negotiation and declaring themselves a failure for not winning a championship. Instead, they (or their agents) will roll out a long list of stats, maybe even a highlight reel, to underscore the value they should command: That, despite not winning, they're successful at what *they* do in *their* role.

You see? Success isn't so easy to define. What's more, by taking an "all-or-nothing" approach to defining or, in the case of leadership, even *evaluating* success, you may jeopardize progress.

There are many layers of success—individual, team, division, organizational, to name a few. There are also levels of progress that would be considered success, and all these levels are worthy of acknowledgment and even celebration.

Late in the 2022 season, Major League Baseball's Houston Astros clinched their division title. There are six divisions. They were still a few weeks away from post-season play, yet there they were, celebrating this milestone by showering each other with champagne after the game.

Oh, and you know each player on that team (and their respective agents) will make note of their contributions to achieving the American League West Division Championship.

Recently, in a refreshing shift from this all-or-nothing view, Giannis Antetokounmpo, a Greek-Nigerian professional basketball player for the NBA's Milwaukee Bucks, shared his views on success and failure. He responded to a reporter's question about whether an early exit from the playoffs meant that his season should be viewed as a failure.

> Antetokounmpo: "You asked me the same question last year, Eric. Do you get a promotion every year? Or a new job? No, right? So every year you work, it's a failure. Yes or no?"
>
> Reporter: "No."
>
> Antetokounmpo: "Every year you work, you work towards something—towards a goal, which is to get a promotion, to be able to take

care of your family, to be able to provide a house for them or take care of your parents. You work toward a go—(stops mid-sentence)—it's not a failure, it's steps to success.

"There's always steps to it. You know, Michael Jordan played 15 years, won six championships, the other nine years was a failure? That's what you're telling me. No, I'm asking you a question. Yes or no?"

Reporter: "No."

Antetokounmpo: "So why [did] you ask me that question? It's a wrong question. There is no failure in sports. You know, there's good days, bad days. Some days you are able to be successful, some days you are not. Some days it's your turn, some days it's not your turn. And that's what sports are about. You don't always win. This year, somebody else is gonna win. Simple as that. We're gonna come back next year, try to be better, try to build good habits, try to play better, not have a 10-day stretch with bad basketball, and hopefully we can win a championship."

Giannis' statements received mixed reviews among some of the league's old guard who still take a more hardline view of success and failure. However, many current players agreed with him. Their more nuanced view recognizes success as not simply an end goal, but as an iterative process, a series of steps, built over time.

The way in which we define success varies wildly according to our personal circumstances and, of course, our goals.

Success on *your* terms

The word success is loaded. It can conjure a whole spectrum of images. Perhaps the title of this book, *Success Frames*, even enticed you to buy it. Using "success" in the title may evoke an image for some people. It's different for us all, but there are common themes we share.

The *first* images that pop up might be anchored in some level of professional accomplishment. Achieving recognition for one's artistic ability or physical mastery and the awards we bestow to acknowledge them, such as an Oscar or Tony Award. Perhaps your image of success is an Olympic gold medal or winning the World Cup (I'm not the biggest soccer fan, but hey, it's the most watched sports event on the planet). Other images that come to mind might involve the achievement of financial success and the excesses displayed as a result.

If we're honest, most of us associate success with these levels of achievement, at least initially. After all, that's what gets all the press. We have lists of the richest people in the world. Entire networks are built around celebrating sports and athletic achievement. And maybe you measure your own success on those same terms. Maybe you've even achieved that level of success. *Hey Oprah. Thanks for reading along.*

However, in our daily lives most people define success quite differently. In 2019, Populace, a think tank founded by Harvard Professor Todd Rose, released the results of a 5,242-person study called the Success Index. The results weren't at all what they expected. In fact, they were so surprised they ran the study multiple times.

The results that surprised them the most were the gaps between what participants thought *others* were concerned with—power, money, status—and how they *personally* defined success. The top three areas participants identified as *their* definitions of success were education, relationships, and character. It's interesting to note that the participants ranged from age 18 to 70.

People clearly define their personal success on different terms than what typically gets celebrated. For our purposes, and one of the reasons this book exists, this is a reminder that *you get to define what success means to you.*

Populace's study points to this as well. If these are the things we truly care about—education, relationships, and character—we may want to celebrate or at least acknowledge this. There are *many* examples of success we can draw from in our daily lives. However, we may not always take credit for them or recognize their significance.

Here are a few that come to mind:

- Learning a second language
- Learning an instrument

- Getting a job
- Buying a car
- Buying your first home
- Losing weight
- Completing a 5k
- Getting a part in a musical
- Making the team

These successes are underappreciated. There's a process, a story behind each one that I'm most interested in uncovering with you. Because it's those seemingly small decisions made each day or each week that led to these results.

At some point in your life, I'm guessing you applied for and were hired for a job. The process you went through, each step of the journey, required you to make decisions and take certain actions. Whether you received help from a friend or career coach, the fact remains that *you* were successful in getting hired. That entire process— the decisions and actions—contain elements of *your* "personal success frame for getting hired."

That's just *one* way to tell the story. Let's change the term "getting hired" to something broader. You "successfully communicated to someone with a need that you possess the skills and abilities to address that need and how you can add value to their organization." *That* sounds a lot like sales and marketing to me.

Your process for "getting a job" has now become something even more useful. Sure, the steps may be different, the product may be different, but by identifying each step, with a few adjustments, it can easily become a framework for selling, or networking, or business development.

These decisions and the actions we take, when stacked together, form the critical elements of our personal Success Frames.

So, why do we look for what's wrong?

T. Berry Brazelton was a pediatrician in Cambridge, Massachusetts. He's most widely known for his Emmy Award-winning PBS show, "What Every Baby Knows", an achievement Dr. Brazelton was very proud to share.

Central to his work with children and families was his developmental framework and his *approach* to working with children and families. The Touchpoints Approach to working with children and families is a set of principles *and* assumptions that, at their core, are strengths-based and always in service of understanding, valuing, and supporting the relationship between the parent and the child.

One such principle encourages early childhood practitioners to "look for opportunities to support mastery," The principles provide a framework for *considering what to do*.

The parent assumptions provide a framework for guiding the way in which we approach working with parents and children, framing up a mindset. For example, the parent assumptions that "all parents have strengths" and "all parents *want* to do well by their child" are meant to help shift the perspective any provider takes when working with a family.

Dr. Jayne Singer is a clinical psychologist with over 40 years of experience in hospitals, schools, and community-based settings. She's also an assistant professor of pediatrics and psychiatry at Harvard Medical School and an international facilitator of the Brazelton Touchpoints Approach and the Newborn Behavioral Observations system. At the Brazelton Touchpoints Center, she spearheaded the Early Care and Education Initiative as an adaptation of the Touchpoints Approach to infuse preventive social-emotional health into early education.

Dr. Singer worked closely with Dr. Brazelton for decades as part of the Brazelton Touchpoints Center and has been instrumental in the development and evolution of the Touchpoints Approach. She shared a story Dr. Brazelton used to tell about his earliest days supervising residents, which illustrates what we miss when we look only at what's wrong.

Early in his career Dr. Brazelton was supervising residents of Harvard Medical School in a well-child clinic. This was before he wrote his Touchpoints books and before he fully developed his Touchpoints Approach to working with families. He was supervising a resident who was conducting a well-child visit with a parent. The parent had come in with their infant and it became clear that there were concerns about "failure to thrive" for the infant.

Failure to thrive is when an infant's weight or rate of weight gain is significantly below that of other children of a similar age and sex. Infants or children that fail to thrive seem to be dramatically smaller or shorter than other children the same age.[1] One of the key components of this diagnosis is determining the cause. It's typically the result of either an underlying medical issue or environmental factors, such as abuse or neglect.

This family also came to the visit with three other, older siblings. Dr. Brazelton observed the resident's visit with the family from behind glass. After the resident had met with a family, they would then come out of the room to discuss their findings with Dr. Brazelton before going back in with the family.

This resident came out and shared a full list of deficits he observed. He mentioned "failure to thrive" and continued to list all the things going wrong with the child and family. Dr. Brazelton was an excellent listener. He listened patiently as the resident listed his concerns, eventually asking Dr. Brazelton, "What should I do about the 'failure to thrive?'"

Dr. Brazelton replied, "Go back in there and find out why the other three children in the family *don't* have failure to thrive. Find out what this mom is doing for them that they are all healthy and thriving."

---

[1] www.hopkinsmedicine.org/health/conditions-and-diseases/failure-to-thrive#:~:text=What%20is%20failure%20to%20thrive, other%20children%20the%20same%20age

The beauty of Dr. Brazelton's encouragement to his resident reveals so much about our obsession with our "culture of failure." In the medical profession and other helping fields, practitioners are trained to look for things to fix. The result of this is to lock doctors into deficit thinking, because, after all, there's clearly something wrong, so the answer must be found in this long list of deficits.

Dr. Brazelton's approach is different. In this moment, he's encouraging his resident to look at the problem through a different lens. This aspect of his approach would later be articulated through his Touchpoints parent assumptions, specifically the assumption that "all parents have strengths."

In this case, the mom has successfully raised three other children who, by all appearances, are healthy. Dr. Brazelton's intention in mentoring this resident is to help him see that learning *how* she did this has value.

Everything's fine

This approach isn't about looking at the world through rose-colored glasses and being blind to what's wrong.

According to Singer, "Touchpoints is built on this premise that we're not ignoring challenges. We're not pretending that challenges don't exist, but the way to tackle those is not head on. The way to tackle those is with a focus on strength."

A strengths-based approach doesn't ignore the issue at hand, in this case the fact that the infant was experiencing a failure to thrive. That was evident. But diagnosing the *cause* of the failure to thrive is what's critical in this moment. That's what will help this child and the family.

By looking for the strengths in this family, this mother and her three thriving children, the resident can explore a key element of the diagnosis: The environmental factors that may or may not be contributing to *this* infant's poor health.

Additionally, in seeking to understand more about the healthy children, the resident can uncover critical information about the daily lives of this family and the three healthy children. Essentially, identifying elements of this mom's *framework for success(ful) parenting.*

And while we don't want to jump to conclusions, having a conversation with the mother about her other children and their apparent good health gives the resident the opportunity to gather more information. In that discovery, he *may* be able to rule out environmental concerns and potentially save time in diagnosing the true cause of the child's failure to thrive.

Dr. Brazelton's Success Frame is his approach. His principles and assumptions aren't simply nice, positive ways to think about a family. The assumptions help to shift our approach to one that looks for the strengths and capabilities within a family. The principles are strategies for building relationships.

In this story there are two assumptions (more, actually) that help frame the resident's mindset as he re-enters the room.

All parents have strengths.

All parents have something critical to share at each developmental stage.

To uncover the "critical information" the parent has to share, Dr. Brazelton is encouraging the resident to utilize two of his principles as a strategy.

Use the behavior of the child as your language.

Look for opportunities to support mastery.

Dr. Brazelton uses the parent assumptions to shift the mindset of the resident to look for the strengths in this parent and recognize they have something *critical* to share that might inform the diagnosis. The strategy for uncovering this information is to talk about the health of the other children, supporting the *mastery* of the parent in raising three healthy children.

All of this is meant to support what's the most important relationship this child will have in their life, the parent/child relationship.

When we adopt a mindset of looking for what's wrong, our deficits or failures, we leave so much on the table. To then make the leap to even considering strengths is challenging at best. However, a strengths-based approach doesn't *ignore* concerns or challenges.

Instead, like the story of the resident, it may serve to identify the cause of the concern more accurately.

In the end, by understanding the strengths of this mother—her track record of successful parenting, her personal approach and framework for successful parenting—this can be utilized and become part of *any* plan to help this infant be healthy.

Core frames

Years ago, my wife and I moved our young family to Maine. At the time, we had two children under the age of four and one more on the way. We both worked, commuting well over an hour each day. My wife managed a call center, and I owned a business with a few partners.

The toll of these long days put a strain and stress on our young family. My wife attempted to mitigate that stress by successfully negotiating a four-day work week. While it enabled her to be home with our boys more often, it wasn't enough.

Eventually, we decided to pursue a different lifestyle entirely. Our goal was to pare back and for one of us to remain home with our children. So, we decided to move to Maine. Between February and May of that year I sold my business, we sold our home, Megin left her position, I found a new position as the executive director of a non-profit, and we moved to Maine.

A few months later we welcomed our third child and bought a new home, where we lived for nearly 12 years. In the span of one year, we (intentionally) turned our lives upside-down and began to craft the life we truly wanted. We also intentionally cut our income in half to make this happen.

When I reflect on that period in our lives, the lessons I extract are all anchored in my (and our) personal definitions of success. However, as you can imagine, that was an incredibly stressful year.

Interestingly, not long after we were settled into our new life, a social worker friend shared with me that the list of everything our family went through in that period would qualify us as being "at-risk."

1. We lived in four different homes in a 10-month period.
2. We *each* lost our job.
3. We had a new child.
4. Our income was cut in half.

There were many setbacks along the way. For example, I didn't get the first job I applied for, or even the second. But the lessons from that period didn't come from our failures. They came from *how* we managed to accomplish what we set out to do.

Of course, it wasn't just *one* decision, it was a series of many small, deliberate steps that made it all work. And it has become a source of many of my own personal Success Frames. Yet, from the outside, it could clearly be viewed as a collection of deficits in need of fixing.

Success multiplies

Approaching anything with a focus on fixing our deficits leaves us with nothing upon which to build. To be clear, it's not as though failure has *nothing* to offer. However, the lessons we generally hope to extract from our failures require a counterpoint of success.

Resilience and persistence, for example, are admirable traits that are typically associated with having experienced a setback. But the lesson of persistence requires a continued effort resulting in some level of reward, a feeling of accomplishment. It's through the lens of that accomplishment that we can extract those lessons. The real gold, though, comes not just from character traits such as persistence and resilience. It comes from pairing *those* traits with an understanding of *how* we persisted.

In the example I shared of moving our family to Maine and getting a job, the whole process was very deliberate and none of it involved simply submitting my resume. Every interview I had was the result of a series of conversations starting with people I knew, then asking and expanding until I found the right person. Here's a short version of what worked.

- Clarifying the role I was seeking and why.
- Developing an elevator pitch version of the role, the why, and how my experience lined up.
- Identifying a list of 10 people in my network who would help.

- Calling them to connect, share my goal, and ask for their advice and help, connecting me with anyone who might also be helpful.

In the end it wasn't the rejections or failures that fueled my effort, it was the small wins gathered along my journey. Each success gave me confidence for my next attempt and bolstered the framework I was constructing. Each attempt got me closer and multiplied my opportunities. Even when I was unsuccessful, I knew that all the steps I took leading up to that point were becoming something I could replicate.

Failure is failing us. It won't serve us well to attempt to extract meaningful lessons from falling short. It's merely a moment, pointing out where things went wrong. The lessons of success, however, reveal so much more. They tell us how. They tell us what worked.

The first step in developing a framework for success starts by looking at what worked for us before, to understand what we might need to achieve success again.

CHAPTER 2

SHIFTING TO WHAT WORKS —SUCCESS IS INCLUSIVE

There has been a significant cultural shift in the last several years calling for a more inclusive approach to solving problems at all levels. This has extended to the workplace, which is evident in the number of diversity, equity, and inclusion efforts and the creation of new positions at the highest levels of corporations across the world. One core element of inclusion is valuing and understanding the lived experience of everyone.

Anthony Barrows is a managing partner at Project Evident and founder of the Center for Behavioral Design and Social Justice. As a behavioral scientist, Barrows has begun calling on his own field to better value the lived experience of those most affected by the problems that behavioral science may be attempting to solve. Barrows isn't just proposing a more inclusive approach but points out how lived experience can *inform* the scientific process by "avoiding obvious mistakes."

> "Having a teammate with lived experience cannot substitute for good (and current) contextual reconnaissance, but it can help teams come up with better insights more quickly. Importantly, it can also help avoid obvious

mistakes made by teams composed completely of outsiders. And all of that should add up to better solutions."[2]

Attempting to solve a problem such as poverty or food insecurity will be aided when the process involves learning from the lived experience of people who grew up in those circumstances.

In their book, *Switch: How to Change Things When Change is Hard*, Chip and Dan Heath outline a framework for change. One of the key components of their framework is to "find the bright spots." To illustrate this, they share a story of Jerry Sternin from Save the Children. Sternin was asked to address the issue of malnutrition among children in Vietnam.

As you might imagine, malnutrition is a complex issue rooted in poverty and limited access to clean water, sanitation, and education. However, rather than focusing his efforts on those larger challenges, Sternin took a different approach, one that sought the lived experience of those he hoped to help. He and his team traveled to the rural villages to have conversations with the mothers and gather data. As they reviewed their findings, his team discovered several instances where even in the most impoverished communities there were families with well-nourished children.

This discovery of "bright spots" rooted in the lived experience of a community revealed a few key

---

[2] https://behavioralscientist.org/lived-experience-makes-the-work-better/

differences in the way those families fed their children. Specifically, the families of well-nourished children fed their children four times a day, rather than the more traditional two meals. Sternin's team also discovered that the mothers added different foods, gathering small shrimp and crabs, and mixing these with the rice they fed their children.

What emerged from Sternin's discovery was a solution to the challenge of malnutrition that was borne from the experience of the people who lived there. Rather than imposing a solution by, as Barrow noted, a team "composed completely of outsiders" relying only on models of behavioral science intended to change behavior, Sternin was not only able to "avoid obvious mistakes" but effectively and more immediately address the challenge of malnutrition successfully. Sternin and his team looked for examples of success to address a challenge of failed nutrition.

As is the case with many not-for-profit organizations, Save the Children recognized a problem, a failure that caused children to become malnourished. This failure pointed to *what* and *where* the problem was. However, failure didn't reveal the solution. Examples of success mined directly from the community of people most impacted, their lived experience, provided a framework for *how* to address the problem.

This Success Frame not only achieved the desired outcome but, in all likelihood, was far more sustainable because it emerged from the community it was meant to serve.

What Barrow is proposing is, in his own words, "not a new phenomenon." And he rightfully encourages organizations to not only "hire differently" but to create a culture within an organization that allows for safety in sharing this lived experience in a way that's valued.

> "The field of behavioral science need(s) more folks with lived expertise. We could avoid so many of the difficulties if the world of applied behavioral science were simply more representative of the world outside: the full gamut of socioeconomic and educational backgrounds, the whole spectrum of gender expression and sexual orientation, the entire array of racial and ethnic identities. Imagine how much better our collective output would be if folks like me weren't squandering our cognitive resources on thinking about how to navigate this stuff. Imagine how much better our insights would be if there were a wider assortment of experiences to rely on. Imagine the different kinds of interventions we might design if our teams were more intimately familiar with the problems we are trying to solve."

Sternin's team and their approach identified an existing Success Frame within the rural communities of Vietnam. Barrow's encouragement to value lived experience and Sternin's approach in finding success within a community are both examples of Success Frames themselves.

Faced with the challenge of fighting poverty, Barrow's experience in applied behavioral science has identified a key component of *his* Success Frame: Including people with lived experience maximizes the impact.

In Barrow's case, a key component is to look for examples of success and leverage them to address challenges.

Let's look at *another* of Dr. T. Berry Brazelton's parent assumptions. We previously identified Dr. Brazelton's assumption, "all parents have strengths" and how the assumptions are helpful in shifting the mindset of someone as they approach working with a family. Now let's talk about the *first* parent assumption in his Touchpoints Approach: The parent is the expert on their child.

Imagine, if you will, a highly trained pediatrician emerging from a top school, having completed residencies in the best children's hospitals under some of the best doctors in the world *and* a mountain of student loan debt. *Kidding. Not kidding.*

For years she's been praised by everyone around her for her knowledge, expertise, and competence. She clearly knows her stuff and has garnered a reputation as one of the most sought-after young pediatricians.

As she enters the room to meet with a new, concerned parent and their child, there's an immediate power imbalance. In the context of a hospital, or even an office visit, the doctor is immediately positioned as the expert, but on what exactly? Pediatrics is the easy, and correct, answer. However, being an expert in the field of pediatrics does have limitations.

As a doctor she relies on information from her patients to make the best diagnosis. In the case of a young child, this information must come from someone who knows the child best, someone with expertise on this *specific* child. In other words, both the doctor and the parent enter the room as experts in their own right and each relies on the other to help the child.

By operating from the assumption that the *parent* is the expert, the doctor and parent can construct an understanding of the child's needs together. Including parents in the process opens the door for more information and a more informed diagnosis.

What these examples demonstrate is a shift from focusing on deficits to one that assumes strength. Beyond that each example *values* a person's expertise through their "lived experience." And by looking for strengths and valuing an individual's experience, we find solutions rooted in that experience.

The way in which we begin to identify these solutions starts with looking for them in the first place and listening to the stories to find examples of success.

Strengths and the stories of our success

If you've ever attempted a significant change in your diet or attempted to incorporate a fitness habit into your life, you've no doubt experienced failure. We all manage to ride the wave of change for a few weeks or even months. We're pushed forward by the excitement and the belief that "this time will be different."

After a short time, we begin to *feel* the effects of our new, healthy lifestyle. We sleep better and have more energy. We talk about it with our friends and bask in the glow of compliments about how much healthier we look.

A few months go by, and things are going well until *something* happens. Maybe we travel for work, or we're caught unaware by an important deadline at work and our new routine gets thrown off. Perhaps we don't have access to the same food or our gym. It could be that a time crunch left us without time for shopping. It's in these moments we start to let things go for a few days and give in to temptation.

The streak we *were* on is now broken. And sure, we might tell ourselves we'll restart in a few days, but a few days turns into a week. Slowly, our old habits creep back in and we've "failed."

Sound familiar? It does to me as well. But here's the question: How often do we examine failures like these for a lesson? More importantly, what would examining that failure teach us?

In this moment, two things are clear:

1. We made a significant change in our lifestyle and sustained our effort for 10 weeks.

2. Something happened to cause our streak to break, and we stopped entirely.

Where should you invest your time and attention? Will we learn more from our failure to follow through or are there more important lessons to be learned from our 10 weeks of maintaining a consistent effort and successfully transforming our lifestyle and body?

In my work with clients, I'm far less interested in what went wrong. I want to know how they managed to maintain their efforts for 10 weeks. How did they get to the gym everyday? How did they resist temptation? How did they consistently eat the right foods?

This is where I want them to look first, for a few reasons. I want to *leverage the emotions of success* as a starting point for understanding *how* this person accomplished a 10-week streak of eating healthily and improving their fitness. Dissecting what we did *well* by talking about our accomplishments is far easier. It's a lot more interesting to share our process and, with the right questions, easier to talk about all the time and effort we put into maintaining our efforts. And, as Fishbach's study suggests, it's a lot easier on our ego.

Let's look at some of the answers to the three questions I posed and some possible answers.

How did you get to the gym everyday?

I need to have everything ready in the morning. So, I purchased two identical gym bags, two complete, identical sets of workout gear, and two water bottles. I pack both bags, fill two water bottles, and put them both in the refrigerator.

I have two days of clothing packed and ready to go.

On the first day, when I get home from my workout, I bring my bag to the laundry room to empty it.

On the second day, when I get home from my workout, I bring my bag to the laundry room and wash everything from both days. That night I wash and refill both water bottles and repack both bags for the next two days.

How did you manage to resist temptation?

I completely removed all the tempting foods from my pantry and refrigerator. If they're not easily accessible, I can't eat them.

How did you consistently eat the right foods?

I found a meal plan online that would help me reach my goals. Then, I made shopping lists each time I went to the grocery store. I have a rule that I can only buy what's on the list. This helps me to avoid impulse purchases and stick to my plan.

Since I removed all the tempting "bad" food, I restocked my refrigerator and pantry with healthier options. Also, just like my system for washing and restocking my clothing so it will be ready when I need it, I started preparing my meals ahead of time.

Every three days I prepare, cook, and pack my lunches and dinners for the next three days. Breakfast is always the same for me and I eat that at home. Lunch and dinner are harder. Lunch is tricky because it's too easy (and very tempting) to buy a meal from someplace close by. Dinner is hard too because I'm often tired at the end of the day, so having meals prepared and packed ahead of time helps me to make better choices each day.

By anchoring ourselves in our success, in the actions we took to do well, we can soften the blow to our ego. Additionally, a study by Gallup found that by focusing on what they do well, their strengths, employee engagement and performance increased significantly.[3] It also increases retention by up to 73%.

What does failure offer?

Let me be clear, it's possible to learn from our failures. Failure points us to what specifically went wrong. It can point us to where the issue lies in a process, for example.

In the case of the health and fitness routine, our failing may point us to a moment where the systems we had in

---

[3] www.gallup.com/learning/248405/strengths-development-coaching.aspx

place faltered. Here's where failure is somewhat useful, as it points us to a moment when the systems failed. In the above example, it happened when the person left the general confines of their home-gym-work routine.

What failure *doesn't* offer is a framework for *how* to address this challenge. The answers for developing a plan for addressing the issue exist in the story of being consistent for 10 weeks.

Small practical steps

My friend Becky McCray works with small towns and rural communities. Becky and her business partner, Deb Brown, are passionate champions of these communities and the people within them. Their goal is to help rural communities thrive. Their approach to accomplishing this is through a framework Becky developed, called Idea Friendly.

Among the many assets these communities have to offer, researchers have identified one asset that puts small towns in the best position to thrive: Openness to change and openness to outsiders.[4] The Idea Friendly method is specifically built to encourage small towns to welcome new ideas, test them, and build on what works.

The story is all too familiar, maybe even a bit stereotyped, but you know the drill. It goes something

---

[4] www.csmonitor.com/USA/Society/2016/0730/Rural-America-confronts-a-new-class-divide

like this. A once thriving small town relied on one or more large employer, such as a manufacturing facility. These same businesses have employed or sustained entire communities for decades. However, they've all left or shrunk to a size where they no longer fuel the economic engine of a town.

And for decades since, as the employers left, the solution on the lips of every town council member was to find another business to replace the one that left. The bulk of the energy generated from their efforts was also directed at finding and attracting similar businesses and refilling the empty facilities with other manufacturers.

In some cases, this may have worked to some degree. But it only provided a stop-gap measure at best. The problem was so pervasive that the size and scope of any replacement, not to mention the eventual inevitable exodus of the new company, has for many resulted in simply delaying the slow demise of the community.

As towns look to replace what has been lost, energy is often poured into finding a silver bullet (read: big) replacement. Becky and Deb, on the other hand, encourage towns to become Idea Friendly and "take small steps."

Their framework is clear and direct. It's comprised of three elements.

- Gather Your Crowd
- Build Connections
- Take Small Steps

"You **gather your crowd** with a big vision. You start a public discussion about the kind of town you want to live in. You create the public focal point for the kind of positive conversations you want to start.

"You turn a crowd into a capable network through **building connections.** You need to connect your people to each other, so they become more than just a crowd, they become a network. In order to make your people even more capable, you connect them with resources and training.

"You and the crowd accomplish the vision through **small steps**. When you start by taking small steps you make it possible for more people to be involved, you cut down the scale of the vision from huge and scary to small and doable."[5]

It's essentially a Success Frame for developing your small town's Success Frame.

Their Idea Friendly approach goes beyond Heath's example of *finding* bright spots. Idea Friendly encourages people to *create* them in your town.

One key to creating these bright spots, says Becky, is being open to new ideas and welcoming them from new sources. Sometimes this means removing barriers to enable people to test these ideas.

---

[5] https://saveyour.town/idea-friendly-method-explained/

Taking small steps, one of the three core components of the Idea Friendly approach, is primarily about testing these ideas in the smallest way possible without the need to jump through hoops.

One way Becky and Deb work with small towns is to visit them and have conversations. But they don't just talk with the people in small town government and other appointed leaders in the town. They want to hear from everyone. They make it a point to visit with local high school students. After all, one of the most common themes in states with rural populations is concern around brain drain. Towns want to encourage young people to stay or, at least, return after college.

One of the most common laments among young people in rural communities is not having a place to hang out. Even a local donut shop where they could sit and talk after school or meet up with friends on weekends would be great, according to many of the high schoolers.

Reactions to ideas like this, if they even get a reaction, haven't always been..., well, *friendly*. Imagine for a moment a group of high schoolers talking about the idea of having a local donut shop, a business in town where they could meet, have a coffee or hot cocoa, a snack and hang out. Maybe it's a conversation that happens in a classroom one day with one of their teachers. It's not hard to imagine a well-intentioned teacher, maybe one who has been eager to start an "entrepreneurship" class at the high school, getting very excited about this idea. And in their excitement they get permission to start an after-school club with some of the kids.

In their excitement they start talking to the kids about developing a business plan for the donut shop. They set up guest speakers and a woman from the local bank comes in to talk about small business loans and credit and capital. They get a local developer to come in and talk about real estate, finding the right location, and again more loans for buying or building or renovating. Since it's a food service business, the local code enforcement officer comes in to talk about applying for health certificates.

Each guest leaves them with a packet of information and a pile of applications. After all, this is what's required to start a business, right? These are the steps *everyone* has to go through, and these people are helping these kids learn the process.

I don't know about you, but I suddenly went from being excited about an idea to seeing a long list of barriers.

With Idea Friendly, Becky and Deb take a very different approach. They want to test the idea *now*, in its simplest form, and build on what works. In the case of *this* small town the approach looked a bit like this:

> Let's find an abandoned lot where a business used to be.

> Set up a folding table and a few chairs.

> Ask your friends if they have a wagon to carry things. Ask someone else to make a sign.

(Gather your crowd.) Make some coffee, buy some donuts, and on a Friday afternoon host your first "Outdoor Café."

Deb suggests asking a local grocery store to donate the donuts. My hometown grocery store often donates plates, cups, and napkins for small local events. (Build connections.)

While you're hosting the event, sell the donuts and coffee for $1. As people come by to see what's going on, talk to them about the project.

We're hosting our first "Outdoor Café" to give local high schoolers a place to hang out.

Talk it up with friends, family, and anyone who comes by. (Build connections.)

Then, after the fact, the well-intentioned adult who was all too eager to support them can help facilitate a discussion about how it all went.

What did we learn?

What would we do differently?

What ideas can we test next time?

And on it goes. This is how you test ideas, in small, actionable steps.

In the world of gamification, or the psychology of gaming, typically the first two levels of any game are designed to be easy. They're designed to be easier to build a sense of accomplishment, to build momentum and generate interest. Research in the field of behavioral psychology supports this. Many of the games found on your phone, for example, are intentionally designed to give you a sense of accomplishment in the first few levels. This is done to fuel your motivation to continue.

Designers make those initial levels easier to help you understand how the game works, and to keep you engaged. Completing a level is satisfying. And you may notice that, along with completing a level, you might receive a message of encouragement or congratulations. "Nice job!" or "Well done!" pops up on the screen.

As you may expect, each level becomes harder, but only incrementally at first. They want you to gain some ground quickly, so while it may be more difficult, it's not a giant leap. And again, you may get some positive reinforcement that acknowledges your success and the change in difficulty. "Whew! Nice work. That was a tricky one."

These games are giving you small wins. They're helping you to develop strategic frameworks for approaching the next level.

The Idea Friendly method wasn't built on the concept of gamification. It was, however, built on the concept of taking small steps. To do this, Idea Friendly encourages you to turn ideas into "practical steps you can implement right away." The purpose of taking small steps is to help you get some of those early wins and gain momentum.

Structure and freedom

Stermin's efforts to identify *examples of success* (well-nourished children) in a rural community requires deliberately choosing to look for strengths within the community. Brazelton's encouragement to his resident required a similar approach, to look for strengths in the family. Both approaches require a few key assumptions. And yes, we must let go of the old adage about what happens when we "assume."

The first is to assume that, regardless of what might be presenting, there's strength, expertise, and, in the case of Stermin's charge, examples of families in rural communities who have found ways to raise healthy, well-nourished children.

Brazelton's Touchpoints Approach provides a set of principles and assumptions that a framework practitioner can utilize for approaching an interaction with a family. There's a structure that this framework provides, but also tremendous freedom for how to utilize it in a given situation.

If, for example, we take the assumption "all parents have strengths." That alone provides a foundation from which we can operate. And the question becomes: How do we *discover* those strengths? As you might guess, Touchpoints has some principles that guide that effort. The framework of principles and assumptions gives the structure. The way it gets utilized is where freedom and creativity come into play.

Our insistence that we need to learn from failure or that we "discover who we really are in the struggle" is flawed. It's also inherently privileged in that it assumes that the stakes are the same for everyone.

I know I've been fortunate to have the support of so many people in my life and that, should it all come crumbling down around me, I had family and friends who would support me, and help me get back on my feet again. Not everyone has the same opportunity or freedom to fail, much less glean anything useful from the experience.

We need to shift our attention to what works, to support and build on our strengths and our successes as well as those of the people we serve.

CHAPTER 3

FRAMEWORKS, NOT FORMULAS

"Your results may vary," is a line embraced by every legal department and marketing team the world over. It also sums up the inadequacy of formulas quite well. It ranks up there with another marketing classic: "Cascade dishwashing detergent's 'Virtually Spotless'". The real definition of *virtually* being, "not actually."

"Results may vary" or "results not typical" is a way of deliberately telling you that this is *probably not going to work* the way you hope it will. Yet, we elevate formulas for success, whether in sport or business. We believe the hype that by doing things exactly as the formula states, we'll be successful, and we forget that circumstances are different and there are too many variables. We forget that all-important line: "Your results may vary."

Of course, it's the variables that render formulas inadequate. Formulas are often presented as a one-size-fits-all solution to achieving our goals. However, we are, in fact, not all the same size. More to the point, our circumstances and abilities vary wildly. Formulas are often too prescriptive, and the circumstances under which they're developed are unlikely to be replicated.

There's no formula for success, personally or professionally. The variations and combinations of situations, circumstances, skills, and strengths are too numerous to boil down to a simple formula. The rigid nature of formulas leaves no room for those variations or accommodations.

Even McDonald's famously simple line: "Would you like fries with that?" which for years dominated the experience of every transaction, won't work 100% of the time, although McDonald's would probably argue it worked well enough to call it a success.

In the world of sports, coaches, teammates, conditions, age, skillsets, are variables that make following a strict formula and replicating success incredibly difficult. Of course, you and I aren't looking to become National Football League (NFL) quarterbacks. Well, I'm not. But many people look for a silver bullet, or at least a formula we can follow.

A common example of how formulas fail comes from the world of multi-level marketing (MLM), also called network marketing. MLM is a business built on recruiting others into the business (downlines) to sell products. For each sale a downline makes, a percentage is earned by the person who recruited them (uplines). The formula for recruiting is scripted and new recruits are trained in how to present this business opportunity to potential recruits. Follow the script, recruit more downlines, make more money. That's the idea.

However, according to the United States Federal Trade Commission, MLM has a failure rate of 99%. Research conducted by Jon Taylor concluded that "On average, one in 545 is likely to have profited after subtracting expenses, and 997 out of 1,000 individuals involved with an MLM lose money (not including time invested)."[6] This isn't a commentary about the legitimacy of these organizations, although that too has been called into question. What makes MLM such a striking failure for most people drawn to the idea is its strict adherence to a formula.

Granted, it works just fine for the organization, given that the industry as a whole grossed $35.4 billion in 2018.[7] But if we look at the individual sellers, the place most trip up is in the adherence to and execution of the very strict formula required for success.

Maybe you've participated in MLM. If not, perhaps you've received a message from a friend or family member inviting you to try some of their products, noting the benefits they've experienced from using them. You may also have noticed that the "invitation" didn't quite sound like them. Maybe it happened at a family gathering where your cousin clumsily shifted the conversation to the new health supplements

---

[6] https://centerforinquiry.org/wp-content/uploads/sites/33/quackwatch/taylor.pdf
[7] www.prnewswire.com/news-releases/new-survey-reveals-73-percent-of-people-who-participate-in-network-marketing-opportunities-lose-money-or-make-no-money-300727716.html

they've been taking and how life-changing it had been for them. Or you may have been tagged in a post on social media.

Again, I'm not denigrating *anyone* who has done this. It's a brave thing. But that clumsy, almost tortured messaging is the *direct* result of being instructed to follow a very strict "proven" formula with little to no variation.

What these scripts end up sounding like is a rather inauthentic communication. This is primarily because, in the end, the goal isn't necessarily to help the person with their health journey. It's designed to extend the business to another level to generate income for those further up, and ultimately the business as a whole.

The training each new person is given is built around insisting on adherence to the sales formula. But what if those charged with coaching found ways to help *adapt* the scripts to each person's strengths? What if, instead of following a rigid formula, they taught individuals a framework based on a set of principles that could be adapted from scenario to scenario? Maybe that first awkward email to 10 family members would look and feel different.

Frameworks are solid enough to provide structure. They may even have foundational principles upon which they've been built. And the beauty of a framework is that it allows room for customization. Frameworks can be used in a variety of situations and, insofar as the basic rules or principles holding them up remain, they can be adapted and expanded.

Developing a framework for approaching our challenges is more sustainable and, ultimately, more inclusive by accommodating individual differences and utilizing our unique strengths to achieve an outcome.

I wasn't the best student growing up. At least not in the traditional sense of getting top marks or class rank. That said, I do think of myself as reasonably intelligent. I enjoy learning and have always been able to understand concepts quite easily but following a specific formula or showing my work felt like a chore.

Looking back, I've realized that, at times, it was excruciating to be required to do things with such rigid requirements. And what I now know is that this frustration was directly tied to my neurodivergence, specifically ADHD, something I wouldn't be diagnosed with until I was in my early 40s.

Being required to follow specific formulas was confining. Being prescribed steps and ensuring each item was complete and recorded stifled my creativity and squashed my interest in learning subjects that could have been truly fascinating.

But I'm not advocating the absence of *any* structure.

Frameworks, not formulas

While rigid formulas can be confining, frameworks, on the other hand, provide structure while remaining adaptable to different needs and different circumstances. With a framework, I can build structures that support *me* and the way in which I work best. More to the point, you can use them to build support structures for the way in which *you* work best.

There are generally accepted principles for building a house. They also come in a variety of styles, forms, and sizes. However, regardless of the style, each home emerges from a core framework: Foundations, walls and supports, considerations for flow and functionality, and a roof to keep it all covered.

It's not that formulas *can't* work. It's just that they rarely consider *individual* circumstances. They're fragile. One misstep and they can fall apart. And the blame, if it should fail, is typically on you for not following the formula.

Frameworks are different. They ensure the structural integrity necessary, while leaving room for customization. A frame supports and allows you to design something specific to the needs of the people who live there.

Of course, sometimes we *are* hoping for a silver bullet, so we look to formulas. We desperately want to know precisely how to replicate the success to which we aspire. If I do x and y, I *should* get the same results. What we fail to recognize is the importance of context. Or, more specifically, the unique nature of the context in which success was achieved and by whom.

How can we replicate the steps if the conditions are different? A formula that worked in one set of circumstances may not work in all environments. In fact, it's likely it won't work in the same way. Otherwise, *every* NFL quarterback would have seven Super Bowl rings. *Hey TB12. Thanks for reading along.*

Musicians improvise from a frame

There are, of course, rules in music. And there are great musicians who have pushed the boundaries and challenged our understanding of what's possible. But these same creative geniuses don't create masterpieces from nothing. Instead, they all start by operating from the framework.

They, more than anyone, understand the composition within the frames deeply. They use them over and over to get to the edges. They find the muse tucked in the spaces between the frames, unleashing their creativity for everyone to hear.

But it all starts with the frame. The components that, when consistently applied, provide enough structure to successfully hold everything together.

Components of a Success Frame

The components of a Success Frame, *your* Success Frame begin by recognizing what worked in a given situation. From that you can identify specific components that, more often than not, will support and guide you to a successful outcome.

It's been said that "the best predictor of future performance is past behavior." In this case we're looking for examples of success. Our goal in reflecting on our past *successful* performance is to identify the components underlying our behavior and guiding our decisions and actions.

In a recent coaching call with a client, we were discussing a challenging situation that involved negotiating responsibility for cost overruns on a large project. To make matters worse, this came at a time of major economic uncertainty. The costs were significant, and the stakes were high. Another consideration was the opportunity for additional, also significant, projects in the future. It was a unique situation and tensions were high. As we discussed how to approach this challenge, we identified two important components of his past successes: "My relationships are the most important thing to me, and I try to be direct."

- Value the relationship
- Be direct

To be clear, these two components are not an entire framework. But they're foundational. They also don't guarantee success. Our success frames are not failproof. What they do is put us in the best position for achieving success again.

In this case, these two components become rules of engagement or principles that guide our actions. But we can't stop there; we must think about *what that looks like in action* to operationalize it.

Your principles and rules are a framework

The notion that we operate from a set of principles is often accepted with a nod of agreement. Of course, we have certain principles that we all believe we wouldn't violate.

It's quite different to turn those principles into a set of guidelines for how we operate and make decisions, and not just those we deem large or significant. The type of in-the-moment decision-making about what we choose to say and do, as well as how we might react, emerges from our principles too.

Operating from a set of principles in this way is an excellent example of a framework. Using principles to guide your behavior, actions, and responses can impact outcomes dramatically.

Given the strict adherence to formulas in the world of MLM, rarely are the reasons for each step explained. There's no attempt to get to the why of the behavior that uplines ask their teams to engage in.

Let's *reframe* the approach to reaching out to those friends and family members using a principle based on how important your relationships are to you and to them. "Value and understand your relationship with the buyer." This is one possible principle in a larger framework for how you might engage with potential buyers.

The challenge with principles lies in operationalizing them to changing circumstances. Interestingly, it's also the benefit. The beauty of frameworks built on principles is that, unlike a formula, they're capable of adapting to new and changing circumstances without violating the principle itself.

Here it is again: "Value and understand your relationship with the buyer."

How might your approach to "selling" or "recruiting" change if you enter each conversation with that principle in mind? Let's break it down by looking at the elements of the principle.

"Value your relationship…" This elevates the importance of the relationship. The relationship we have with the person to whom we're selling has value. Therefore, we would do nothing to harm it. Quite the opposite. If we value the relationship and the person, we shift from looking out for *our* interests or the interests of the company we represent, to one that has the best interests of the buyer at heart.

"Understand your relationship…" This helps us to think about the context of the relationship. What's it based on? What are our shared interests? What does this person value? What do I understand about this person's interests and needs?

When we approach selling with that mindset, with the mindset of *valuing and understanding our relationship with the buyer*, we may think differently about how we frame the conversation.

You can see how, operating with even just this *one* principle in mind, instead of following a strict script, you might be able to have a conversation, construct an email, or some other outreach that's more personal, relevant, and authentic. At the very least, you may not put the relationship at risk, recounting a very impersonal, inauthentic, script.

Of course, this isn't easy. Taking the time to think about how you might say something versus using a template that you've been assured is "proven" feels safer. The problem is that the "uplines" aren't always interested in your individual success insofar as it conflicts with the directive. And, in the end, it's also easier to fault the person *implementing* the formula than to say the formula doesn't work. After all, they've trotted out their top sellers at conferences, the 0.05% of those who have made $100,000 or more by "following the formula." So, while it's working for some, the data shows it's not many.

One of my early personal criticisms of Stephen Covey's *7 Habits of Highly Effective People* was that it wasn't operational, that it lacked context or instruction. Of course, what I was looking for was a formula for what to say or do. Now, my "critique" might be that Covey's "7 Habits" aren't habits at all. They're principles.

Let's compare the principle I used above with two of Covey's.

- Principle #4: Think Win-Win = Value the Relationship
- Principle #5: Seek First to Understand, then to be Understood = Understand the Relationship.

What I appreciate about Covey's two examples is that they clearly honor the other person, but also honor our own needs as well, which of course is necessary.

Sometimes, when we think about "valuing our relationship" with someone, the focus tends to fall on the other person. But that's only half the story. Relationships are by their nature interconnected. We must value ourselves within the relationship too.

Just a quick note. I cringed a bit and considered leaving out the Covey example because it felt dated and surely he's received enough accolades over the years, but it was such an excellent example, I couldn't ignore it. So, if you rolled your eyes at yet another Covey reference… same here.

Gatorade and Kobe were on to something

"Be Like Mike" travels well. It's easy to carry. You can do with it what you please. It's a bit broad, but in some ways it resembles a principle and could be part of a framework for success. Naturally, Gatorade wanted you to keep one part of your approach connected to their brand and the *thing* they wanted you to carry was their beverage.

Beyond consuming the same drink that Mike drinks, "Be Like Mike" begs us to ask: What are the principles or rules that guide Michael Jordan's behavior and put him in the best position for success?

Likewise, Kobe Bryant's "Mamba Mentality" isn't a formula and, at least for Kobe, could be a principle or a collection of them. If you Google the term, you'll find numerous definitions, quotes from Kobe himself explaining how this overarching idea becomes a set of operating principles, and a framework for his success:

- A constant quest to be the best version of oneself
- To live with a purposeful intensity

What these principles meant to Kobe, in his career as an athlete and in his life outside the game, are different than they would be for you and me. Herein lies the beauty of a framework, especially one rooted in principles. It allows you to consider what it means and what it looks like for *you*.

Play from center, wait on the bounce

In another lifetime, I played the game of squash. I remember two distinct lessons that immediately changed the way I approached the game. As a novice, I was forever chasing down shots and doing my best to return the ball as quickly as possible. This was fine if I played against someone of similar skill, and I managed to win some games playing this way.

One day, a guy, who a friend and I affectionately nicknamed "The Cannibal," asked me for a game. He proceeded to humiliate me by making me dart all over that 32' x 21' court. Afterwards though, he offered to coach me.

Play from center

My first lesson was one of those moments when you think to yourself, "I can't believe he's making me do something so simple." The Cannibal had me stand in the center of the court with my arms outstretched. Between the length of my arm and the length of the racquet I was able to reach more than half the distance to the side wall. He then asked me to take one big step, and I've covered the entire gap from where I was standing to the side wall. That's it. One step and I reached the wall.

Similarly, a few steps diagonally forward or back and I was able reach the corners. What was once an exhausting attempt to cover 672 square feet of court was now reduced to a few deliberate steps in any direction.

And after each swing, he had me return to center.

Wait on the bounce

Squash balls are deceiving. They don't bounce like a typical rubber ball. Initially they appear to ricochet all over the place. However, after hitting the wall, their velocity decreases and once they hit the floor their bounce is deadened even further.

So, rather than rushing to return a serve immediately after it hits the front wall, you wait. You look for that moment after the second bounce when the ball appears to hang in the air for a split second. And then you swing.

Playing from center puts you in the best position from which to take action.

Waiting on the bounce gives you the time (the space between) to choose where you want to direct your next shot.

And this is what good coaches do well. When it feels like you're constantly reacting and chasing balls all over the place, they help you see the game differently. They help you find the space between so you can choose how best to respond. And they help you return to center and put you in the best position to make the right moves for whatever comes next.

There's a quote attributed to psychiatrist and holocaust survivor Victor Frankl:

> "Between Stimulus and Response, there is a space. In that space is our power to choose our response. In our response lies our growth and our freedom."

It's in this space where we can consider our actions. This space is also where, often in a split second, we can think about *how* we want to apply a principle.

It's hard not to see how Frankl's quote resembles the two principles I gained from my squash coach. *Waiting on the bounce* is all about finding the right space between stimulus and response, and *playing from the center* puts me in the best position to do that.

The framework, guided by the principle, allows us to adapt to situations and find success on our own terms.

Preparation and practice—a framework

I've always loathed role-playing. You know the drill. You're in a workshop learning a new approach and the instructor invites you to act out a scenario. It has always felt awkward and inauthentic. And we tend to think, "It would never really go like that." All of which justifies our dislike. *Just me?*

"Prepared and practiced"

I'm borrowing this from my friend Kate, who shared this perfect phrase on a Mastermind call. We were talking about confidence. She helped articulate the distinction between being prepared and being practiced. And the value of ensuring we do both.

Simply put, if you're preparing to give a presentation, it's essential to have all your slides, supporting data, and notes in order. And there's some amount of confidence that comes from that preparation.

However, your knowledge on a topic may not always translate to giving a convincing presentation or conveying your point on that same topic. Speaking is a skill that requires practice. At its most basic, there's timing to consider. Pacing and phrasing are important. There are pitfalls to avoid and ways to improve our ability to communicate. Practicing helps cut those awkward umms and uhs that plague so many of us.

One of my common mistakes has been forgetting or not trusting what's on the upcoming slides. My brain is always trying to anticipate. I worry I'm going to miss something. To make sure I don't forget, I slip and mention a point too soon in the presentation. I'm reminded of this when the slide I *prepared* precisely for that purpose shows up two slides later.

Practice would have helped me avoid this.

Practice is an act of service

Maybe you don't often present. However, I'm guessing there are other opportunities. Perhaps you call it testing or walking through a sequence of events to ensure everything flows as it should. Regardless of what you call it, that step, finding ways to practice, is an act of service to the people you serve. In addition to improving our confidence, it demonstrates a level of care for your clients.

Let's turn this into a simple, repeatable, and adaptable framework for improving your confidence in whatever you're developing.

- Prepare: Gather your information and build everything you need
- Practice: Rehearse, review, test, walk it through
- Polish: Spend more time on the parts that need tightening
- Present: Deliver the product or presentation to your audience

This framework comes from having experienced successful presentations and deconstructing the experiences and everything that led up to them. I know that I benefit from being prepared and practiced, no matter what I do.

I could say the same about running a 10k. I'm going to perform better if I:

- *Prepare* for the race by having everything I need on hand
- *Practice* running to build my endurance
- *Polish* the important parts of the race (sprint finish, well-paced start)
- *Present* my best performance on race day

This is a consistent, repeatable, and adaptable framework that provides me with my best shot at a successful outcome.

Everything benefits from a frame

One of the benefits of a good Success Frame can be its ability to be reused or applied to a variety of circumstances and by many people, regardless of their situation.

Often, when we think about the military, a word that often accompanies it is *precision*. As you might imagine, however, the variables that need to be considered when making a decision and choosing an action are numerous. Add to that the life-and-death nature of many of those decisions and the stakes are extraordinarily high.

The most successful military strategy (according to a strategy contest) is one called the OODA loop. It looks like this:

- O – Observe
- O – Orient
- D – Decide
- A – Act

Observe: Where am I right now? What's going on?

Orient: Okay, that's where I am. Here's my approach. I'll orient myself to this approach (get in alignment with it).

Decide: Here's the path I'm taking.

Act: I'm doing this. I'm executing on things. I'm taking action.

This military strategy is a framework for successfully navigating yourself and the people you're leading through a situation. It's not a specific formula, in that it doesn't *instruct* you on precisely what to do or how to respond. It does what a framework should do, it supports you in a challenging situation. Each element of the frame slows you down, encourages you to not just react or respond immediately to the situation. Instead, it provides a structure for us to sit in the space between stimulus and response, taking in information before we decide and take action.

The usefulness of frames

Jon Swanson is a hospital chaplain. Before that he was a pastor at two churches, but many people know him through his writing at 300wordsaday.com.

Jon has been writing and sharing his thoughts online for nearly two decades. He was an early adopter of social media and formed many connections on Twitter in its earliest days, which led to him becoming known as the "Social Media Chaplain."

His writing, and more specifically his kind, thoughtful approach, has helped people all over the world, many of whom, with no religious upbringing, think about their faith in new ways. It's this same thoughtfulness, combined with his intellect and profound empathy, that's helping so many people reshape their understanding of grief, and how we might support those experiencing loss.

As a hospital chaplain Jon has a front-row seat to the impact of loss on the people left behind. As you might imagine, it's difficult to know what to say, much less do, in those situations. How does one comfort a parent who just lost their child?

Reframing grief

Jon wrote a book called *This Is Hard: What I Say When a Loved One Dies*. The title alone reflects Jon's thoughtfulness and gentle precision.

How did *you* read the title? Where did you put the emphasis?

Jon's first chapter ends with three possible versions.

- *This* is hard.
- This *is* hard.
- This is *hard*.

One three-word phrase with so many possibilities. This is what it looks like to frame things. It guides us while leaving room to make it your own.

After all, as Jon says in his introduction, "No one has ever had this moment after this death of this person. And no one will again."

And what about the subtitle? I'll be honest, my mind read it wrong. In my head, I heard, "What *to* say when a loved one dies." And here's the subtle beauty that reveals Jon's approach. The word "to" *could* seem helpful initially; after all, we do crave answers in moments like this. But grief isn't that simple, and Jon understands that taking a prescriptive approach dismisses the unique nature of each loss, the complexity of our emotions, and the weight they carry.

Instead, by saying "I," Jon frames a conversation about grief that acknowledges the difficulty, while opening us up to consider not just what he says, but what he *considers* before he says (or does) anything.

Among his many encouragements, one that resonated with me was to "remember the best time, not the last time." This one gentle, intentional phrase reframes and reorients us. It gives us permission to look through a different lens, to look for the best, whatever that may be.

What follows throughout his book are examples of what he, in fact, does say to people experiencing grief. Each careful phrase manages to acknowledge the unique personal impact, the fact that it is indeed hard, as well as illustrating the expectations with which we sometimes burden ourselves.

As someone who is experiencing grief as I write this, and likely still as you read this, his approach has reframed my understanding of grief and unburdened me from those expectations.

Habit framing

I have six simple habits that sum up most of my days:

- Start
- Finish
- Eat
- Sleep
- Move
- Connect

That's it.

Of course, each habit encompasses more than one word. Connect, for example, serves as a reminder to make time for my family, talk with my mother a few times each week, call a friend, connect and engage with people online, and make time and space for personal reflection.

But, for me, there's one habit that serves as the linchpin for everything else. It, too, comprises more elements than one single word: *Finish.*

The most effective habit for framing up success each day is to end the day well. To be clear, I'm not talking about finishing as a means of closure or completion. For me, "finish" is about setting myself up to have everything I need for the best day tomorrow.

Finishing my day by going to bed on time means I'm more likely to get the *sleep* I need.

Finishing my workday by reviewing and writing out my plan for tomorrow means I'll *start* the next day well.

Finishing my night by tidying up the kitchen or something as simple as programming the coffee maker means I wake up to fresh coffee and a clean place to cook my breakfast, so I'm more likely to *eat* well.

Finishing my day by deciding what I'll do tomorrow for exercise and getting any gear I need ready means I'll *move* more.

Finishing my day by making time and space in my schedule for a walk with my daughter or a phone call with a friend means I'll honor the importance of these relationships and *connect* with the people.

I like the process of taking a few moments at the end of a long day to ask myself, "What do you need tomorrow?"

For me, finishing isn't about pushing through the pain of the last mile of a marathon, proud of my grit and determination. It's about going to bed the night before knowing I've done everything I can to have the best race possible.

Frameworks unlock our creativity

We rarely benefit from a one-size-fits-all approach. Simply put, there are too many factors at play to take a prescriptive approach to achieving success in a certain area.

- Context
- Natural strengths and abilities
- Motivations
- Goals
- Past experiences

Your business isn't the same as mine. Even if it were, we may not be at the same point in its growth and evolution. As such, it doesn't make sense to assume we know exactly what you need. It doesn't make sense to teach you a rigid formula to follow.

What *does* make sense is to understand who you are, who you serve, and how you serve them. It makes sense to understand *your* goals for *your* business. It makes sense to *know* you.

What I'm certain of, however, is that everything benefits from having a framework. Not least of which is that by identifying the frameworks that support us, we can unleash our creativity.

There are things we all need to do each day that don't require our creative energy. However, I still hear from folks who approach even the most routine parts of their day at their whim. They dip in and out of emails without a plan. They approach projects as their mood dictates and treat mundane tasks as creative endeavors.

All this saps our energy. But the freedom we seek, the creativity we crave as we approach everything as it suits us, can actually be found when we apply a bit of structure in the form of a frame. Creativity is at the service of discipline, and the mundane is dispatched by the same.

When we approach tasks with simple methods and consistent execution, we minimize the draining impact. In addition, it allows us to bring creativity to our business and life. Let's not waste our ideas and inspiration on things that don't merit that gift. Instead, let's build frameworks to be creative where it matters.

The central challenge of approaching success as a formula to follow is our loss of humanity. We're not machines capable of replicating actions with the precision required of the exacting standards of executing a formula. We're flawed. We're nuanced. We don't operate in a vacuum.

At their core, Success Frames help us to *reclaim* that humanity. Our own, and in our relationships with others.

PART II

RECLAIMING OUR HUMANITY

CHAPTER 4

CREATE SPACE—DON'T GRIEVE THE GRIND

Our celebration of the hustle and grind is harming us *and* our organizations. Of course, there's nothing wrong with working hard, but there's a false notion that hard work naturally leads to professional (and/or financial) success.

Beyond that, "hard work" is often equated with "time spent working" and thus we celebrate the person who is the first to arrive and the last to leave. What we *don't* talk about are the costs associated with adopting a lifestyle that places work above all else.

As an individual, you may decide that it's worth the cost. But as a leader in an organization, it's clear that creating a culture around this mindset and expecting everyone in your company to adopt the same mindset is no longer viable. We need to let go of the idea that the level of sacrifice required is worth the *supposed* success it brings.

It's entirely possible that the drive for professional and financial success is worth the cost for some. You may be perfectly fine with staying late and missing out on dinners with your family or attending your child's events, choosing to honor your family in a different way. Or you may be in a position where time with family isn't even a consideration, affording you the ability to put in long hours.

However, applying that standard to an entire workforce of individuals whose backgrounds, circumstances, cultural or personal values differ wildly, is far from equitable or inclusive.

A wake-up call

The Covid-19 pandemic brought about seismic shifts in the way we approach work. Companies were forced to adopt the idea of remote work, providing employees with a new perspective.

Removed from a regular routine for a significant amount of time, this afforded many the opportunity to reflect on their relationship with their employers. And many came to realize that some of those costs, essentially in exchange for a paycheck and benefits, may no longer be worth it. People no longer needed to devote hours each morning simply getting ready for the day. Whether that meant the need to adjust schedules based on traffic in preparation for a long commute or meeting the requirements of professional dress.

This was especially true for women, upon whom the responsibilities at home fall disproportionately in contrast to their opposite gender partners.[8] Add to that

---

[8] https://news.gallup.com/poll/283979/women-handle-main-household-tasks.aspx

the expectations for what constitutes professional dress for women in the workplace, it places extraordinary additional pressure and cost, particularly in the form of time.

The pandemic also reframed many aspects of leadership and management. Beyond the impact it had on corporations shifting the way in which they conducted business, employees themselves reevaluated *their* approach to work and what it means to exchange their time for a paycheck and benefits.

"The times they are a changin'."

24 hours

This is hard. Those are the comforting words my friend Jon Swanson shared with me after my brother-in-law passed away suddenly and unexpectedly.[9] Or maybe he said, "This *is* hard." He may have also said, "This is *hard*." Grief is a strange thing. Each version of his words is helpful at different times. Time looks different during grief. In fact, time looks different for many reasons.

There's a phrase I'm guilty of using over the years that goes something like this: "We all have the same 24 hours. It's how you use them that matters." Have you heard it?

Some versions of this phrase are shared across social media platforms, often by aspiring motivational

---

[9] https://300wordsaday.com

influencers. Each one has convinced themselves that their relentless drive and hustle mentality is the key to their success. And they want to convince you of the same.

I've come to dislike this phrase—a lot. And it isn't just the loss of someone I loved that caused me to rethink what I now see as its harmful impact.

No, we don't *all* have the same 24 hours in a day. It may be true that we exist in a world where one day is measured by a 24-hour period, but those 24 hours look very different for each person. For example, if a person with physical limitations needs 45 minutes to do something that takes *me* only 15, we don't have the same amount of available time.

In the wake of our family's grief, even with my day carefully planned, using my best time management framework, I frequently found myself staring off at nothing for long periods. One morning shortly after his passing, I spent an hour with my wife, crying together. We talked about the deep pain of this loss and the echoes of past grief it has conjured.

If you've experienced grief, you understand that time looks different for us in those moments. Different than it did just a few weeks before.

My wife and I each own our own business. We work from home. For several weeks, work and business looked different. And we were okay with that. It's also worth noting that we were *fortunate and privileged to be okay with that*. However, things we would typically complete in a few hours might take a few days. Grief affected everything, especially our time.

It's hard not to get caught in the trap of inspirational platitudes. There's a reason they catch on and get shared. We may at times even find them motivating, causing us to rethink how we're using our available time. And there's nothing wrong with that. However, adopting it as a universal truth is not only wrong, it's harmful.

So, while technically the world operates on a 24-hour clock, each person does *not* have the same 24 hours. And sometimes it's because, as my friend Jon says, "This is *hard*."[10]

But it's not just in grief or having a disability that affects our relationship with time. A recent fun and clever experiment by *Glamour* magazine illustrated how different men and women experience time. I share this example fully aware that this study is only talking about gender in the binary. However, it's a useful example of the impact of time on certain segments of the population. Perhaps it will also illustrate yet another pitfall of maintaining these strict distinctions.

Glamour magazine compared various "*shared*" routines and experiences encountered by men and women, from

---

[10] www.amazon.com/This-Hard-What-When-Loved/dp/ B0939M9R6M/ref=tmm_pap_swatch_0?_encoding=UTF8&qid= 1664989991&sr=8-1&inf_contact_key=9fff91716c8bb61383df- f2e449c4f991f651f238aa2edbb9c8b7cff03e0b16a0

the time they woke up and throughout the day.[11] This included even seemingly small moments throughout the day. One example was the difference in time spent shampooing hair. It turns out that women spend one minute more than men shampooing their hair. Trust me, it adds up. In this case, it adds up to more than six hours a year. Truthfully, I was surprised it wasn't more.

In the end, this study demonstrated that to "be a woman" in modern society takes *15 more days each year* than to "be a man." Over a year, women have 4.1% *less* time available to them compared to men. And in case you think this is simply a matter of "how they use their time,"16 hours of that additional time is simply time spent *waiting in line for the bathroom*.

The impact of this hour by hour means that for every 60 minutes available to men, women have only 57.5 minutes to accomplish the same task. In a nine-hour workday, women lose nearly 23 minutes.

And again, a person with physical limitations must approach *their* time differently, setting aside additional time to get ready for work or additional time getting to and from. That extra time has a cost that may come in the form of less sleep, less time with family, or any number of other activities required to rest and replenish before the next workday.

We simply do not all have the *same* 24 hours! Using phrases such as "we all have the same 24 hours" fails

---

[11] https://hellogiggles.com/time-takes-woman-man/

to acknowledge any position of privilege from which we may benefit, or any conversation about the cost, or tradeoffs we might be able to make to achieve our definition of success.

Acknowledging reality

In the past few years, a theme has begun to bubble up that, at the very least, has received *meme status*. Whether it permeates beyond that remains to be seen. The phrase goes something like this: "Be kind. You never know what someone is going through."

I don't know whether my interpretation of this is correct, but I take it to mean that we should give each other a little grace, even if the other person is disengaged or curt with us. They may be experiencing something— grief, financial struggles, food insecurity, a divorce, physical pain, or emotional pain, just to name a few.

Again, I'm not sure how *well* we practice this level of understanding, but it's nice to see it in the conversation.

I've always had high expectations of myself. And I've, most certainly, fallen short of those expectations. That said, yet another popular quote meant to inspire is the phrase "no excuses." I'm not a proponent of the "no excuses" mindset. At least in the way it often gets applied. The chants of "no excuses" may feel motivating in the short term, but they often ignore the *reality* of our circumstances.

I don't know whether you follow the game of golf. I don't actually keep up with it but I do watch whenever there's a major tournament. As I sometimes do, I had it on in the background the other day but perked up when I heard an interview with one of the top golfers in the world, Justin Rose.

During one of golf's major championships, Rose faltered and dropped out of contention within a very short time. In his post-match interview, he reflected on the day and on his performance. He noted that he started to "lose his concentration."

"I felt like it got very distracting. I felt like the crowds were thinning out. Everyone was on their way home. There was a lot of movement off the ball. So, you know, shadows were lengthening. There was a lot to deal with, contend with coming down the stretch."

Quite frankly, it sounded like he was making excuses and blaming external factors for his poor play. After all, movement, conversation, distracting shadows all seem like part of what you sign up for as a professional golfer. But he didn't stop there.

Rose went on to say, "But I wasn't able to deal with it very well." In that one sentence, his list of excuses became a statement of the realities he had to contend with. And he took ownership of his performance in the face of those circumstances.

One of the reasons I don't like the #noexcuses mindset is that it sometimes glosses over the reality of the circumstances we face. When we acknowledge reality, we're not making excuses. If we're afraid that we're making excuses because we recognize and consider the obstacles around us, we could miss out on taking complete stock of our situation. If we're afraid that we're making excuses, we might think the answer to every challenge is to "work harder" or "grind it out."

We are, as Justin Rose did, making a note of what's going on around us. We're observing, gaining insight and clarity so we can become better at figuring out "how to deal with it."

Creating space

A while back I found myself with a block of "waiting room" time. It was the type of waiting that required you to be nearby for an undetermined duration, *just in case*. And it might last an hour... *or three*.

I don't know about you, but I'm not terribly patient in these situations. I prefer a little definition to my day. Of course, I immediately began thinking about ways to make use of every minute. What could I accomplish with all this time? After all, I wouldn't want it to go to waste.

My list grew quickly as I contemplated running a few errands nearby, squeezing everything I could out of the moment. And then I just stopped, let all of it go, and took some of the time to enjoy the silence.

Silence and stillness are not unproductive

That's the way we tend to view silence. We're often uncomfortable with it. Try spending 20 minutes in your car with the radio off. Better yet, count how many times you reach for the knob. Try leaving your phone in your pocket while you stand in line at the store. Or just try waiting, in silence, for anything for more than 15 minutes.

We're always looking for distractions to fill the silence. So, we pull out our phones and check... something. I do it all the time. I've even advocated using these moments to be more productive by replying to a few emails, for example. But sometimes silence is an accomplishment.

The fact is that our brains need this time. We need moments where our minds wander and our focus gets a bit fuzzy. That's where connections are made and ideas emerge, in the quiet spaces in between. And they come when we stop looking for every distraction available to us to fill a void.

Just do what?

My good friend Sheri's favorite phrase is: "Don't just do something. Stand there."

Of course, we're *always* looking to "just do *something.*" Nike's famous tagline "Just Do It™" isn't particularly helpful if we get stuck on "Just Do" when we're not terribly clear about what "It" is.

And that's where silence comes in, because when we stop doing, even for a few moments, our "it" tends to reveal itself. Maybe your silence is prayer or meditation. Maybe you just focus on your breathing. Maybe you stare in wonder at a spiderweb or the night sky in late summer. The point is to stop. The point is to sit and wait in silence.

When we're constantly told to *hustle* to be successful, it can be hard to allow for those moments. But I promise you they're as important as anything on your to-do list.

My waiting room silence didn't last the entire time. It didn't need to. But the time I *did* spend, felt good. It cleared my mind and eventually I eased back into a few simple things. I emerged less harried and grateful for those moments and my ability to recognize them and choose silence.

The value of stepping away

Have you ever found yourself stuck on a problem and can't find the solution? Just me?

In those moments, my brain goes a little haywire. The frustration starts to build. I may even get angry. Mostly because I *know* the answer is right in front of me. I just can't see it.

I used to get caught in a bit of a tug-of-war in those moments around approaching this. On the one hand, I felt compelled to persist. But, on the other hand, I knew

I needed a break. A voice in my head would tell me to *just work harder* and *grind it out*, that there's *honor in the struggle*. There was a very loud voice telling me there's a *lack* of honor if I walk away.

Eventually, though, my frustration reaches a point where I *need* to step away. Without fail, maybe an hour or a day, or sometimes a week later, a solution pops into my head, and I'm able to fix the issue.

Research supports this idea. While we may not be working on the problem directly, stepping away allows our subconscious mind to take over while our conscious mind takes a bit of a respite.

Get some distance

In the simplest terms, our brains become exhausted from working on the problem. Grinding it out isn't likely to help in that regard. So, giving our minds some space and relief allows room for creative ideas to emerge.

I approach these situations differently now. I've turned it into an essential component of my Success Frame for *whenever* I get stuck. When I recognize the frustration building, I step away from the problem. For me, it's not about creating the space to think about the problem. I need to let go of working directly on the problem for a while and trust that an idea for a better approach will come to me.

Sometimes it's what we're thinking about that gives us new ideas. My friend Chris Brogan has always encouraged people to read books that have *nothing* to do with their industry to generate new ideas and inspiration.

> "When someone is frustrated with their role, my advice always is that they learn something new. You never fail anyone by learning more. It doesn't always line up to what you want next or what you even need, but it's learning. It's never wasted... Learn whatever is NOT about your current role and current situation."

If you're in sales and things are a bit flat, picking up the latest book on "7 figure selling" may not be as helpful as reading something entirely different, such as Abdi Nor Iftin's memoir, *Call me American.*[12]

Recognize those moments when you need to step away from the problem and perhaps think about something entirely different. After all, you're not likely to solve the problem by sheer force of will.

The challenge of time—an exercise

Not only do we not "have the same 24 hours in a day," but there's a tendency to underestimate the amount of time we have to accomplish a goal.

I've used the phrase "your day, is your week, is your month, is your year" for awhile now. It's meant to be a simple and effective method for looking at your annual

---

[12] www.callmeamerican.com/

goals and breaking them down to identify the daily actions required to achieve them.

If, for example, you hope to generate $120,000 in annual revenue, that works out to be roughly $10,000 a month or, more accurately, $2,309 per week. And we can continue to drill down to arrive at a daily plan of action for achieving that.

But I want to add some nuance to this approach. What do you want it to look like? Our goal is to find space in all the busyness and reclaim control over where you direct your time and attention. Our work isn't always about an end result. More specifically, as we pursue those results, we get to choose what we want our year (and every day between) to look like.

However, in doing that, we don't always account for the time we want to spend outside of work, at least not first. We know there will be holidays and vacations. We know there will be times when we're busier and times when things slow down. But we don't always approach our planning with that in mind. By not considering the variances, our expectations for what we can accomplish over a period of time are skewed.

Is it really 52?

I wrote the numbers 1 through 52 on a sheet of paper. Next to each number, I wrote the corresponding date for each week of the year. I began blocking off weeks in which I wanted to spend time completely away from work with family and friends on vacation or holidays.

I noted weeks when my children are on school break. During these weeks I like to have a lighter work schedule. I looked at the seasonal ebbs and flows of our lives, such as when we begin and end the school year to help our kids transition. These weeks tend to be a bit disruptive for everyone until we settle into our new routine.

After taking all that into account, I was left with 36 full weeks. Even then, some weeks were less full than others. I didn't note weeks in which there was a Monday holiday, for example. The result was that 36 weeks is a very different number to work with than 52.

Here's what I found most helpful about this exercise:

- My annual planning prioritizes time with my family. I decided ahead of time to set aside significant time for that.
- Many of the other weeks (holidays, school vacation, weeks of transition) will happen regardless. By planning *for* them, I can plan *around* them.
- As I look at the results I want for my year, I now have a clear and more accurate picture of the time resources available to commit to achieving them. Thirty-six weeks, in fact.

Looking at the revenue goal example, with only 36 full weeks to work, I now need to generate $3,333 each full working week.

To be clear, it's not that I don't work on some of those school vacation or transition weeks. I do, however, schedule them differently. I don't count on having the same level of focus or productivity.

And then what happens? The next step for me is to look at the typical seasonal fluctuations of our business. There are times throughout the year when, at least in our experience, people tend to disengage, and business slows down.

In the case of my wife's photography business, there are months when she doesn't take pictures at all. Megin shoots mostly outdoors. We live in Maine. Business changes in the winter. Likewise, her late summer schedule is packed with senior photos. These are a few of her seasons.

All businesses have seasons, and when we know them, we can plan accordingly. And, of course, we all need to make time for ourselves or our family.

Start there and see what you're really working with.

Adapting this exercise: My wife and I are both self-employed. We have a great deal of flexibility with our schedules. The result might look different if I worked in a corporate setting, but the approach would be essentially the same. Within the confines of my role, I would look carefully at my available time off, the holidays that are recognized in the organization, and my understanding of the seasonal ebbs and flows of the organization. Then, I would go through the same process. For me, that still means beginning by prioritizing time with my family. For a simple template of this exercise, visit robhatch.com/52

Ultimately, we want to both acknowledge the realities of the limited resource of our time and relationship to it. And as we build frameworks to support how we choose to utilize that time, I hope we can also acknowledge that others may not share the same reality.

CHAPTER 5

DECONSTRUCTING THE STORIES OF OUR SUCCESS

Not every Success Frame is personally constructed. We learn, we borrow, we adopt, we test, and develop our own Success Frames by noticing what works and adding it to our repertoire.

A Success Frame is a series of operations and conditions supported by specific actions that typically lead to a successful outcome:

- Operations—what you do
- Conditions—what you need
- Actions—how you do it

We've all been successful at something. The story of how you scored high marks in particular subjects has more to tell us than your failing grades.

- How did you get your last job?
- What did you do to land your biggest client?
- How did you lose weight?
- What enabled you to stick to that exercise program?

The stories of our accomplishments contain critical elements. They reveal how and why we're successful and how to do it again.

One of the key components of anchoring yourself or others in their success is to help support resilience. When faced with adversity or setback, something we all experience, having a mindset of resilience, what Carol Dweck would call a growth mindset, is key.

> "In the fixed mindset, everything is about the outcome. If you fail—or if you're not the best—it's all been wasted. The growth mindset allows people to value what they're doing regardless of the outcome. They're tackling problems, charting new courses, working on important issues. Maybe they haven't found the cure for cancer, but the search was deeply meaningful."
> – Carol S. Dweck, Mindset: The New Psychology of Success

Success is rooted in our resilience, our ability to try again in the face of failure. But sometimes we get so caught up in what isn't going well that it's hard to see what's working.

Keep the receipts

The city of Milnor, North Dakota has a population of 700 people. Carol Peterson is the city's Economic Development Coordinator. Like many small communities throughout the United States, Milnor has experienced its fair share of change over the years.

For many of these communities, these changes come in the form of economic setbacks. Long-standing employers, key engines for the local economy, may choose to leave the area. It should come as no surprise that in a rural community there are people who will comment on the fact that:

- There are too many empty buildings
- No one wants to live here anymore
- There are no new businesses
- More businesses are closing

Let's not get into the fact that these same folks will drive to the next town over to visit a Walmart and hit the McDonald's drive-through instead of patronizing local businesses, but I digress.

In her tenure as Economic Development Director, Carol Peterson has experienced these naysayers firsthand. People who continually voice their belief that no progress is being made.

"I continually hear from community members (the naysayers) that we don't ever get anywhere, we are at a dead-end… but I have the ammunition to counter these people with my data.

"We have 25 businesses today that we did not have 12 years ago, some being anchor businesses with a number of employees such as our electrical/HVAC with 15 employees, veterinarian with 4 full time and 6 part-time, childcare center with 16 employees, plumber with 5 employees.

"If we don't keep track of this info, soon no one has the information to show how we have grown."

The examples above are just a small slice of the growth Milnor has experienced in the 12 years since she took her role. Peterson continually documents and updates the city's successes.

"If everyone would keep track of what they are doing, they will be very surprised what they have accomplished."

Her document provides a succinct summary of:

- New businesses
- Public improvements
- Business expansions
- Business successions
- Business remodels/new builds
- Improvements

Under the list of improvements, she cites four awards her city has received over a seven-year period as a result:

- 2021 Healthy, Vibrant Community Award
- 2020 Main Street Smart Infrastructure Award
- 2019 Main Street Excellence Award
- 2014 City of the Year Award

Peterson's advice to new economic developers is to "keep track of what grants they have received." It was advice she received herself that has proven incredibly useful.

"I would not believe how many grants we have received if I had not actually recorded the dollars brought in and where they came from. Milnor has received over $2.3 million in grants since 2010!"

According to Peterson, these are all grants awarded from the state and don't include an extensive list of grants from foundations as well. And yes, she keeps track of those too.

This is how she responded to those comments and the negative perceptions her town faces, even from the people who live there. She keeps the receipts.

In Idea Friendly terms, it's a list of things people have tried to create the town they want. More specifically, this long list is a story of people who found ways to test ideas in small, but significant steps. And by reminding people of all the great things happening in their town, it becomes a new version of the Idea Friendly principle of "gather your crowd," insofar as it can become a new rallying cry for what's possible.

This is also an example of not just *finding* the bright spots but continuing to remind people that they exist, even if they may not always see them. And just to be sure that members of the community *do* see the list, Peterson makes a point of publishing her list in the local paper a few times each year. Sharing the success stories of her small city is one way she reshapes people's perception or, at least, counters some of the negativity that often spreads like wildfire.

Deconstructing our stories of success must start with making note of them in the first place.

Why is it so hard to celebrate the wins?

Is it just me? I know it's not, but I'll own it. A friend congratulated me on a recent accomplishment and asked me about it. I politely said, "Thank you." I did share more with him, but I kept it short. Apparently, my dumb brain didn't want to show in any way that I might have enjoyed the recognition or, worse, come off as full of myself. So, I said something to downplay it or get through the story quickly.

But *he* asked *me*! He started the conversation by congratulating me! Still, my mind is screaming at me to stop talking, that he doesn't want to hear about it and is just being polite. So, because I'm uncomfortable with accepting praise or appearing overly proud of an accomplishment, I end up devaluing his interest. I'm dismissing a friend expressing heartfelt congratulations.

There's a profound difference between being proud and telling everyone how wonderful you are. I think we fear that the former automatically leads to the latter. Or, at least, that people will perceive it as such. That worry gets in our way, so we clam up, deflect, and downplay the importance of the recognition.

But honestly, that achievement represents something. Maybe you got a promotion. Perhaps you landed a client or booked your first speaking gig. Each one of those has significance. It's a recognition of hours of hard work and persistence.

When someone says congratulations, take a moment to enjoy it as an acknowledgment of their genuine congratulations and recognition of all you did to make it happen. They could be pointing out a great example of a Success Frame.

Tally your wins

I'm willing to bet that you've had some wins this year. I'm guessing there's something you've done consistently for the past several months that has resulted in a success you wouldn't have achieved otherwise.

I encourage this a lot with others and, quite frankly, with myself. There are certain times when people start to scramble a bit. They're trying to hit goals they haven't met. They beat themselves up for all the intentions they set that never became a reality. They wonder where all the time went and how they got so far off course.

However, it's possible that we haven't veered as much as we think. It's easy to recall all the things we think we should have done, but I'm not sure it's beneficial. We know that focusing on areas where we fell short isn't all that instructive. And much like Carol Peterson's experience in Milnor, it also doesn't tell the whole story.

Maybe you didn't complete the 10k you signed up for, but you did train consistently for eight weeks. Maybe you didn't hit your sales goal, but you still managed to increase revenue by 10% over last year.

Sometimes our accomplishments aren't even connected to the goals we set. Things change, and maybe you made adjustments you weren't anticipating. You quit a job. You got a job. You started a business. You made new friends. You learned two new songs on the guitar you found at a yard sale. And yes, maybe you set out to learn 10, but now you know two that you didn't know before.

It's what I'm supposed to do. Sometimes our "accomplishments" are things we might consider obligations when, in reality, they too are worth acknowledging:

- You helped your child through their first year of college
- You paid 25% more in sales tax this year because your business grew
- You took a vacation with your family
- You coached your child's basketball team

Sometimes our accomplishments are incomplete.

- You wrote 30,000 words of your book
- You lost 10 pounds
- You created content twice a week

Maybe it wasn't exactly the progress you hoped you would make. However, you have a choice in how you want to view things. It can become a list of having successfully made progress or a collection of negativity highlighting what you didn't finish.

Count the small stuff

As you look back at the last year, take some time to tally your wins. Look at the small stuff. Look at the everyday moments when you played games with your daughter or reorganized your spare room. We overlook those things because they don't feel big enough to celebrate.

It could be something simple:

- You landed your first client (or three) in a business you started
- You launched a new product or service
- You've lost weight
- You're fitter than you were six months ago
- You filed your taxes on time this year
- You cut your debt in half
- You got a new job
- You spent more time with your kids or significant other

Whatever your win might be, it's likely a result of deciding to do something different or choosing to stop doing something, and... it stuck.

I'm pretty sure the person you were 12 months ago had their doubts. They weren't sure you would make it. But here you are. You've chalked up a significant win. And it's worth taking a moment to recognize where you started and what you've accomplished.

So, what was it? What's one win that's a direct result of choices you made months ago?

Revisiting what you know

There are times when we all need a reminder of what works. It's not that we should approach every problem in the same way. However, when things feel a bit out of whack, often it's because I've let my core practices slip a bit.

Recently I've been struggling with transitions. When you work from home, even with dedicated office space, the lines get blurry. Transitioning from one thing to another isn't always a simple process.

In a previous life, my commute served as a way to transition from work, letting go of the day and preparing my mind to be present for my family. I don't have that commute anymore. But I do have a process; I just needed a bit of a reminder.

Part of my process for writing my weekly newsletter, something I've done for over a decade, is to review recent topics. I keep every newsletter I write, titled and dated, in Google docs. As I was searching the topic of transitions, I came across these excerpts from several years ago.

In 2009, business school professor Sophie Leroy wrote a paper titled "Why is it so hard to do my work?" She studied the effects of task switching and discovered that we have what she calls "attention residue." Each time we switch from one thing to the next, we carry with us cognitive remnants of the last task. This residue does indeed negatively impact our productivity and our ability to focus on the next task. How could it not? We're trying to focus on one thing and still thinking about another. We're bound to lose something in the transition.

If we're not focused, we're not thinking clearly. If we're not thinking clearly, we're not making good decisions. This described precisely what I've been struggling with. I've been carrying "attention residue" with me from moment to moment.

And then I found this: When our family sits down for dinner, we say grace. We've done it for nearly 18 years together. We say it every time. Life is hectic. Cooking and preparing a meal for six or more takes a lot of work. Beforehand, we're all busy, and then suddenly we're together. What I notice most during grace is how it helps to slow us down. It encourages a deep breath and connects us with one another as we go around the table one by one. Were we to jump right into eating, I think the harried nature of life would carry over into the meal. Grace is a transition. It sheds what came before it, settles our minds, grounds us, and shifts our focus to each other.

In Jewish tradition, there's a ritual at the end of shiva (the first seven days of mourning). Before entering the next phase, sheloshim, mourners "rise up." They walk around the block or their house, often accompanied by friends. This walk aids in the transition back to everyday life. It symbolizes re-entry into the world. Sheloshim is a transition. Its purpose recognizes that one can't go from the intensity of shiva straight back into our life.

I've often bucked traditions. Being raised Catholic, I found them boring. I once saw the rituals as mindless repetition and rejected them. Because of that, I missed the purpose of rituals. I overlooked their ability to help us shift our thinking. Rituals prepare us and carry us as we move our attention from one thing to the next.

For example, we know that we should stretch before exercising. Triathlons have transition areas between elements. Athletes have a routine for putting on their gear at each one.

Everything points to taking the time to prepare our minds and our body for the important work to come. The purpose of rituals, an experience of their own, is to set us up to focus and shift our attention where it needs to be.

At the time, I really needed to read those. I needed the reminder.

A key component of building our Success Frames is to revisit what we know about a similar situation. We don't always need to learn something new; we just need to remind ourselves of what we already know works for us.

Reflective practice

"It's not the state you're in; it's how you got there." This quote is from the Associate Chair of Psychiatry at

Stanford, David Spiegel. He's talking about something called locus of control.

> "Locus of control refers to the degree to which an individual feels a sense of agency in regard to his or her life. Someone with an internal locus of control will believe that the things that happen to them are greatly influenced by their own abilities, actions, or mistakes." – *Psychology Today*[13]

The more self-directed our efforts, the greater our satisfaction. In other words, the more we're in control, the more autonomy we have in our decisions and actions, the more satisfied we are with the process and the outcome.

Our past success, specifically the decisions we made and the actions we took, are fundamental in identifying the degree to which *we* influenced a successful result.

What did it look like when things went well? This is one of my favorite questions. This is different from imagining an "ideal week" that hasn't happened yet. The goal is to mine your past success. And perhaps more importantly, identify your role in creating the scenarios that enabled success. Or as David Spiegel put it, figuring out "how you got here."

When working with someone, I want to understand their strengths. Not only the strengths that come from an assessment, but real-world examples of their past

---

[13] www.psychologytoday.com/us/basics/locus-control

wins, no matter how big or small. Examining and naming the steps we took to accomplish something has tremendous value. The lessons are in the decisions you made and actions you took to sustain your effort. The lessons are in the conditions you created that enabled a successful outcome.

It's not a specific formula you're looking to extract and replicate. Every situation has nuances that need to be considered. It's about identifying the key pillars, a framework that supported you when you faced a similar challenge. Asking, "what did it look like when this went well?" is a great way to restore our locus of control. It reminds us that what we used to do (sometimes without thinking) was actually a process honed over years of practice.

Sometimes we do things seemingly automatically, and never had to stop to think about each step. But those steps represent a framework. Revisiting "what went well" uncovers our personal framework for success. It helps to ask the right questions. But what *are* the right questions? The right questions are the ones that, when asked, result in an answer that moves you forward in your efforts to become better.

To get to the place where we ask ourselves the right questions, it's important to understand how we learn as adults. One of my favorite quotes is from educational reformer/philosopher John Dewey. Dewey said, "We do not learn from experience... we learn from reflecting on experience." – (*c.* 1933). He was speaking about adult learning, specifically.

Children learn by acting on their world. Adults require some amount of reflection on what they've done to learn from the experience.

Reflective practice is a concept introduced in 1983 by Donald Shon. That's 50 years after John Dewey said those words. This summary from University College Dublin explains reflective practice well:

> "In reflective practice, practitioners engage in a continuous cycle of self-observation and self-evaluation in order to understand their own actions and the reactions they prompt in themselves and in learners.... The goal is not necessarily to address a specific problem or question defined at the outset, as in practitioner, but to observe and refine practice in general on an ongoing basis."[14]

Taking time to review your work and reflect on it must be a regular occurrence, a consistent practice. The "goal" is "not to address a specific problem" but to "observe and refine practice." For our purposes this works. You want to get better.

Productivity icons such as Dale Carnegie, Stephen Covey, and David Allen have, as part of their teachings and methods, made some reference to taking time to reflect, to do a "weekly review" (Allen) or encourage you to "sharpen the saw" (Covey).

---

[14] https://www.ucd.ie/teaching/t4media/reflective_practice_models.pdf

In this context it's an important tool in the process of *creating space between stimulus and response* and directing your attention to the work that matters. The challenge, though, is that it's one thing to accept this as a premise, but it's quite another to be able to put this into practice.

How do we accept positive reactions and acknowledge our shortcomings without giving too much energy to either one?

Our internal dialogue tends to be dichotomous. We generally focus on two questions: What did I do wrong? What did I do well? Unfortunately, as we've learned, we tend to focus on what went wrong disproportionately.

However, the answers we're seeking to get better rarely lie in what went wrong or what isn't working. They lie in asking "what went well?" and more importantly, "why?" and "how do I replicate it?"

We need to move from exhaustively examining our failures to recognizing them and moving through them. We need to focus our efforts on what went well, knowing what success looks like, and understanding how we can replicate it.

"That went well." "Nice job." "That was helpful. Thank you." These are all responses I received after I presented a workshop to a small group of people. They were kind. It was great to hear. Truthfully, it did go well. I know the information was helpful. People left with good information and ideas. However, in the quiet of the car ride home, their words and their reactions became hollow. I started to feel as though I had missed the mark somehow.

Sidenote (and a warning): Many, if not *all* of us, have some amount of post-performance insecurity. To alleviate that, we look for feedback and reassurance from others who have "experienced" what we did to give us perspective. However, most folks are unwilling to be critical, let alone constructively critical with us. Some of this is part of our cultural norms. More importantly though, it's *not their role*. My advice is not to dive too deeply into self-criticism and to simply be grateful for positive reactions without giving too much weight to them. Get some perspective in the form of distance and then evaluate using reflective practice.

So, how do we use reflective practice to get better? One of the reasons reflective practice is so important is that it gives us a way to take stock of what happened and, to some degree, identify our actions *and* the result. Essentially, creating some amount of personal feedback.

Valary Oleinik is a speaker and gamification consultant. She has spent years understanding how to use the psychology of gamification to motivate and engage. Part of the appeal of many of the games we play are the rewards it gives us along the way. Think about the last game you downloaded on your mobile device.

According to Oleinik:

> "A reward is not, 'ring the bell and a prize pops out.' A reward is that you get feedback.

And if you look at rewards that way, it's a very different experience. One of the key things I always tell people when they're starting out with anything gameful is to recognize that if they can make progress visible, magic happens.

We also benefit emotionally and otherwise from mastering something. People like to figure things out. People like puzzles.

They want a little mystery. You want it hard enough that it stays interesting, but you want it easy enough that you can do it.

In games you kind of do that. You do that loop. Stress a little bit. And then, oh, okay. I got it."

Reflective practice, particularly when we look for what went well with a desire to understand what worked and why, is precisely about "making progress visible." It gives us feedback on the strategies we used, the choices we made, and the actions we took.

And it's not just game apps that utilize the psychology of gamification and feedback in the form of rewards. There are apps designed to help us hit our fitness goals. There are apps that monitor our sleep, our nutrition, and our weight loss. If you have a goal, there's probably an app for that. And it likely uses some form of gamification.

For these apps, ensuring that people sustain an effort is key to the company's success. Of course, users abandon those efforts all the time. However, if making progress visible is key to that effort, when someone starts to wane, facing that broken streak can be devastating.

Oleinik says that many of these apps have figured out ways to get people back on track.

> "What apps are now doing is monitoring that. The person is getting ready to fail so I'm going to deliver them some prompts that say, 'Maybe we need to adjust that goal instead of just abandoning ship. Let's take a moment and let's regroup and reset the counter.'"

Fishbach's conclusion that our ego prevents us from learning from failure lines up with this. The app isn't concerned with what went wrong as much as it wants to help you find a way to get back on track, to make your progress visible once again.

Reflective practice isn't simply the act of reflecting but reflecting with the intention of identifying and improving how you do what you do. The process of reflection is, in many ways, about telling the story of what happened.

Chipotle's Success Frame

If you've ever walked into a Chipotle restaurant, even for the first time, it's clear that they've established a process, an order of operations for just about everything. We're going to focus on their ordering process.

- Bowl/burrito/salad
- Brown rice/white

- Pinto beans/black beans
- Chicken/pork/beef
- Salsa (mild/med./hot)

And on it goes down the line. Usually, there's a person who covers each station and each choice. Sometimes one person handles two stations, and they send it on down the line.

Note: Each station has a specific set of rules and actions to be completed.

This is their framework, an order of operations for success burrito building. The result is a remarkably consistent and personalized product. Because *you* helped construct it.

But take note... *they* determined the options available to *you* at each station *and* the order in which you proceed. Once you walk into the store, their *customer frame* funnels you through a very specific set of steps that, combined with their *operations frame,* gives you a tasty meal.

Assembly lines—starting with success

Picture an assembly line. We inherently know its purpose. It was created as a process of efficiently ordering a series of operations, in a line, to consistently produce a product. This is what Chipotle has done. It's what manufacturing plants have done for over a century.

Here's the tricky bit and where we get a little lost. We're probably not making a sandwich we can eat or a car we can drive. The end product *feels* less concrete. But in each case, their process wasn't constructed, it was *de-constructed*.

Success Frames start by identifying what success *looks like*! Then we can look at the steps you took to create success, and build and adjust.

You'll note that I'm not telling you specifically what to do or what each step should consist of; that's up to you and generally works best when you leverage prior success. You're the architect of your Success Frame!

Looking for patterns of your own success

Let's look at an example of the sales process. If you're in insurance sales, you could likely identify who your top clients have been, let's say your top 20% who have likely contributed to 80% of your revenue. This is your tasty burrito.

- Who are they?
- What do they have in common?
- How did you get the sale?
- What were the steps you followed along the way?
- What happened just before they signed the deal?
  - What did you say or do?
  - What did you have prepared?

Focus on what *you* can control.

- And before that, what did you do?

All the way back to how you identified them and qualified them at the very start.

I promise that you'll be able to identify a specific, common set of operations that, when done consistently, in order, will generate a similar successful outcome *more often than not*. I would also be willing to bet that, in your process of deconstructing success, you'll recall people who *could* have been your top clients. You'll also start noticing that the reason they didn't sign with you is most likely because you forgot a step, or in tasty burrito terms, forgot to ask them if they wanted guac?

Leveraging the lessons of unrelated successes

- Getting a job
- Starting a business
- Buying a house
- Losing weight

There are any number of successful outcomes (large and small) we can draw from to inform our frames. Maybe we've packed on a few pounds in the past few months and it's time to get back to fighting weight.

What helped you to lose weight a few years ago? "Well, I was a lot more disciplined a few years ago. So, it was easier." (That's not an answer, by the way, but it's a start and holds a key.)

What helped you be more disciplined? What did it look like? "Well, I had a list of what I could eat and what I couldn't. I prepared my food the night before. I didn't eat ice cream each night."

So, a list, preparation, and no ice cream. How did you avoid eating ice cream? "I didn't buy it in the first place."

So, your list of approved food is what you used to shop? And so on...

This is how we identify the Success Frame for weight loss. And here's how we *leverage* unrelated success...

What would it look like to set up a similar framework for applying for a job? What are the lessons of your success that you could apply to your job search?

Does the process require a similar amount of discipline? Would a list be helpful? What do you need to prepare?

CHAPTER 6

SUCCESS FRAMING—WHAT DO YOU NEED?

What do you need to be successful? What environment best supports you to accomplish your goals?

"Iron may sharpen Iron," but those moments are meant to be brief, not a persistent approach for achieving optimal performance. If the Great Resignation, quiet quitting, and the like have showed us anything, it's that we want work environments that are supportive and allow us to contribute our best work.

Here's where you'll be working. This phrase may sound familiar if you've ever received the bare minimum orientation for a new job. Of course, we understand we may not have a lot of choice regarding where our office or cubicle is situated. The company may have already determined the layout of the office space. They've determined which teams will be situated together and their proximity to supervisors and managers.

But how many employers have asked you what you need to be successful? More specifically, what you need to perform at your best?

Ideally, organizations hire for talent, for what people do well. However well-intentioned, companies don't always extend the conversation about talents to include the *conditions* that facilitate our best performance.

Understanding our personal stories of success shifts our focus to what it looks like when things go well. And part of the process is also to understand the conditions that support you to perform at your highest level.

In an organization, it's the culture that sets the tone. Leaders provide a level of permission, and the opportunity to take risks and fail needs to be encouraged, and a certain amount of forgiveness applied. Part of setting that tone means finding opportunities for employees to not only share their strengths but also providing individuals the best opportunity to use their unique perspectives and talents.

Specifically, the conditions under which they're most likely to be successful.

Context matters—what do you need to be successful?

Traci Sponenberg is the Chief People Officer at The Granite Group, a plumbing and heating, ventilation, and air-conditioning wholesale distributor in New England. In her role, Sponenberg has fostered a "people first" approach to her organization. And while phrases such as "people first" sometimes feel like buzzwords or fads, she and her team, with the *full* support of her CEO, live it.

"I'm a real believer in adapt to the person and adapt your own style to the person instead of taking one philosophy and just pushing that through the organization.

"I'm also a big believer in helping people achieve what they want to achieve and in looking at potential and looking at wrapping development around strengths."

Adapt to the person

Sponenberg is incredibly personable. As a leader in her organization *and* in the field of human resources, she's very present. She holds workshops and gives keynote addresses and interviews. However, contrary to what many people think, even those who work with her, she's an introvert. This has required her to, at times, adapt herself to certain situations. She shared a personal example of what that looks like and how it has shifted communications with *her* boss, the CEO.

Being an introvert:

"… doesn't mean I can't speak. It doesn't mean that I can't be in front of people. I'm actually really good being around people. It means that on a day that I'm having a lot of Zoom calls, I'm gonna do it from home because I'm gonna be really exhausted."

I mentioned that her "people first" approach is shared and supported by the CEO and owner of the company.

"My CEO needed to learn how I work best, and he's still sometimes learning, in that he knows I'm *better* when I can take information and process it over time. He used to just call me and ask, 'What's going on?' Now he says, 'I'll call you at four and let's talk about what's going on.' So, he has learned to sort of adapt *his* style and we need to do that with our people."

This understanding and adapting has extended to the entire company, and influenced the way in which they hire, develop, and promote their employees.

"We need to deeply understand our people, understand their strengths, understand their needs and wants. And then create *with* them, not *for* them, but create *with* them a development path that makes sense for them."

In the past, promotions were generally given to the most senior person at a location, whether it made sense for the company or the employee.

"What we're really trying to do is develop the people skills and put in the best *people* manager. Because some of our best managers are ones that have the *least* knowledge of our products. But they are *extraordinary* people managers."

For The Granite Group, focusing on what employees do well and making them a partner in their professional development process has helped grow the company tremendously over the past few years. Today they're known, even by their competitors, as one of the top companies in the industry to work for.

Accommodations for all

Much like the story of Dr. Brazelton's resident, many people approach the idea of providing accommodations with a view to fixing something, viewing the need through the lens of a deficit.

Sponenberg's personal story of needing time to recover and time to process information is a great example of a company and its leaders *accommodating* someone's working style. The key difference in their approach is that her company doesn't view her need as a deficit that needs fixing or accommodating a weakness. Instead, The Granite Group's "people first" mindset looks at accommodation through the lens of providing what an employee needs, to help support their strengths, and enabling them to give their best performance at work. It's about shifting from a viewpoint that says, "Traci gets tired and needs to rest," to one that says, "Traci performs at her best for our company when she has the time to process and time to recover."

And the importance of companies shifting to an approach that adapts and supports people to perform at their best is becoming more evident every day. In the years between 2007 and 2016 there was an enormous uptick in the recognition and diagnosis of ADHD and autism in adults.[15] Perfectly successful individuals

---

[15] https://behavioralscientist.org/lived-experience-makes-the-work-better/

have gone 30, 40, even 50 years without understanding that the way in which their (our) brains work is quite different from the brains of "neurotypical" individuals.

According to Deloitte, research suggests that teams that include neurodivergent professionals can be 30% more productive than those without neurodivergent members.[16] Through their Autism at Work program, JP Morgan Chase found that cognitively diverse employees are 90% to 140% more productive than neurotypical employees and make fewer errors.[17]

The fact remains, whether diagnosed or not, people with ADHD and other neurodivergent diagnosis, such as autism, often have different needs, specifically as it relates to environment and communication. While no two neurodivergent individuals have the same strengths, abilities, or needs, there are some needs that many share.

For example, they may find excess noise or harsh lighting distracting. They may have difficulty managing interruptions from managers or team members. Their need for communication may also be different. Many folks with a neurodivergent diagnosis prefer clear, consistent, and direct language devoid of the need for interpretation. They benefit from shorter meetings with a clear purpose and agenda. They may require notes after a meeting to help clarify expectations.

---

[16] www2.deloitte.com/us/en/insights/topics/talent/neuro diversity-in-the-workplace.html

[17] www.ft.com/content/ea9ca374-6780-11ea-800d-da70cff6e4d3

Every person's needs are a bit different, and those are just a few examples of the types of environmental supports and accommodations that overlap for many. Just for fun, let's look at that short list again.

- A quiet environment
- Calm lighting
- Reduced interruptions
- Clear, direct communication
- Consistency
- Shorter meetings with a clear agenda
- Clear expectations, written out

Maybe it's me, but those *accommodations* sound a lot less like something we need to do for people with a diagnosed disability and more like a better way of running a business.

As you can imagine, *asking* for what you need requires *understanding* what you need to be successful. So, how do we get there?

As someone who was diagnosed quite late in life (nearly 40) with ADHD, I'm still learning about what works best for me. In my book *Attention!* I shared elements of that, and how I use reflective practice to better understand the conditions.

Stop accepting the default settings—discovering your needs

One of the best results of having been diagnosed with ADHD nearly 10 years ago is how it helped me understand my abilities and needs differently. After nearly a decade of working with coaching clients, I've learned that I prefer to speak with clients via the phone or some other audio format rather than a Zoom-style video call. The *default* is that most clients expect our sessions will use video. While I'm always willing to make that accommodation, I know that I do better with just audio.

As it turns out, this is quite common for folks with ADHD. Even before I understood how this related to *my* ADHD, I used to explain my preference to my clients. I'm an auditory processor and an associative thinker. Using the phone and listening to a client describe a situation allows me to focus and be present with them. I find video to be very distracting and impacts my ability to hear what they're saying.

As I listen, my brain makes mental notes. Something a client says in the first five minutes of a session gets connected with something a client says 20 minutes later. And I pull the threads together. I still explain it this way, it's just that I now understand more about *why* this is.

While I'm always happy to adjust to the needs of my client, and would certainly defer to their preference, my ability to focus on what's being said or to note shifts in tone to discern meaning is easier when I can just focus on their voice.

Additionally, I often pace when I'm on a call. The addition of physical movement supports my ability to remain focused on what's being said. It's also worth noting that by *not* using video and pacing, I'm also further away from my computer screen. So, I don't have to spend any energy on exerting willpower to resist the urge to check something unrelated to the call.

If I worked in an environment that required frequent Zoom meetings, I might request an "accommodation" to be on audio only, perhaps after an initial visual check-in. In both cases, while the request accommodates *my* needs, it's always in *service* to the person on the other end of the call.

Much like Sponenberg's example of needing time to process or to be home during a day of many Zoom meetings, my "accommodation" is very much aligned with being able to perform my best for the work that's required. My clients depend on my ability to focus on what they're saying. They count on me to hear them, not just their words, but to ask questions that uncover intent and meaning to guide and support their thinking. If my ability to do that is diminished by a requirement to be on screen, they may not be getting my full and complete attention.

A note about accommodations: Let me be clear. I can be present on a video call. I can concentrate on the task at hand. However, the energy required is far greater than it would be on audio only. So, there's a cost.

As an example, imagine for a moment you injured your leg and needed to use crutches. You have a meeting with a potential client. You arrive ahead of time, with plenty of time to spare, time to sit, anchor your mindset, review your notes, or whatever you need. When you get there, you discover that the elevator is under repair. The meeting is on the third floor. It's not that you *can't* make it up the stairs, but it will come at a cost.

As you ascend, along with the physical toll, you start to realize you'll be arriving *just* in time for the meeting with nary a moment to spare. Not only have you lost the time you built in, but you can feel yourself straining with each step, and you'll likely arrive sweaty and uncomfortable. This is not the impression you hoped to make.

So, while using the stairs is entirely possible for you, there's a cost. It has an impact on how you show up. One last thing: When you finally arrive, you might take a moment to explain the situation to whomever greets you. They apologize profusely for the state of the elevator and say, "If I had known about your injury, I would have let you know about the elevator ahead of time." Still, they offer you a water and a few minutes to gather yourself in the restroom before the meeting starts. A very kind *accommodation*, if you ask me.

Let's look at something many of us have in common— our phones. At their best, these incredible devices are designed to deliver us information and allow us to communicate with others. At worst, they're addictive. And I don't mean that in a casual sense. Studies have shown that excessive cell phone use can lead to depression and anxiety.[18] And with each new app we

---

[18] www.ncbi.nlm.nih.gov/pmc/articles/PMC6449671/

add, we extend its ability to interrupt and therefore disrupt our focus.

I think of each notification, each red dot, each buzz and ding we allow to enter our consciousness as taking a sliver of our attention. Even if we "ignore" the phone as it buzzes in our pocket in the middle of a conversation, it interrupts our thoughts and we're immediately aware of the need to check. Even if we quietly silence it in our pocket and send the call to voicemail, our brains are already at work processing the possibilities of who it might be.

- I hope that's not important.
- I wonder who it was.
- It was probably spam.
- Oh, I'm expecting a call from my mom. She can wait. Can she wait? She can wait.
- Maybe I'll say I need to use the restroom to get away from this conversation so I can check who called.
- How long do I have to sit here nodding my head to make it look like I'm not doing that?

What if we took a different approach? What if we spent a bit of time designing the experience we have with our phones? What if we set it up to serve our needs? *But I already do that.* Sure, we may take some time to select a ring tone or which apps are on our home screens, but these devices are set to a default that delivers the information the software and media companies *want* you to see. It's your job to fine tune the settings. You have the power to choose *which* pieces of information and from which sources. *You* get to choose who has access to you, and the notifications that arrive or interrupt you.

What do *you* need... to be successful?

Imagine if the person setting up that meeting you "crutched" your way to had asked you this question. Instead of viewing getting there as one part of a test that demonstrates your worth and value to the client, what if they viewed your complete success as equal to their own? What if they called you a few days ahead of time to ensure you had everything you need?

"Is there anything you need to help make this meeting successful, Mr. Hatch? Do you have any needs you would like us to be aware of? We'll be meeting in the third-floor conference room. Unfortunately, our elevator has been out. Are you comfortable using the stairs? We can easily move the meeting to the first floor if that works better for you."

Rob, you're living in a fantasy world. *Maybe.*

Let's go back to the reaction of the person you first encountered. "If I had known about your injury, I would have let you know about the elevator ahead of time." It makes sense. Anyone of us would genuinely feel bad to have put someone through that and, had we known, we might have let the person know. This would have at the very least allowed the person more time to arrive earlier to gather themselves.

Why then wouldn't *we* state our needs ahead of time? Of course, we both know why. It's because for some reason we don't want to appear weak or vulnerable. As though *feats of strength* are part of demonstrating the value we can bring.

But by *not* stating them, we could denying the people we're there for our best performance.

Using the tools you have as an accommodation

Often, I'm asked about which app or piece of software I use to run my business. My answer varies, but when I probe a bit, most people aren't looking for something new, they want to know that what they're using is still okay.

Most small businesses don't have the resources to conduct extensive side-by-side software comparisons. The good news is, more often than not, they're simply not using their current software to its full capacity. With a little guidance and support, the tools you have *could* be all you need.

For many, it's the daily stuff that causes the most headaches—email, calendars, note taking; really, anything having to do with managing time and information is where many people become stuck. There are hundreds of options. You could go blind reading reviews while trying to decide on the best application or platform. However, the secret to all this is far less technical and a lot more human.

What do you need?

Email is a fierce beast to tame. In our overwhelm, we tend to look for new apps to help us fix what's wrong. But we don't always define the problem very well. Feeling overwhelmed by your inbox isn't the problem, it's a symptom. The primary cause is that we don't take the time to go beyond the default settings that come with our email software or any app.

Whether you have Outlook, Gmail, or another platform, each one comes loaded with powerful features. They can deliver email to us when and where we want it. Software, particularly now that "AI has entered the chat," can sort information by level of priority, organize it based on the sender, a subject line, and so many other filters. It can snooze, remind, schedule, and be turned into an event on our calendar.

We essentially have the "robot butler" we dreamed of at our disposal. We just need to tell it what we want it to do. That's the part we so often miss. So, *what do you need*?

We're all very comfortable with setting alarms. We all have moments throughout the day when we need reminders to wake up, do something, or be somewhere. So, we tell our phones what we need, when we need it, and even the tone of the reminder. Somehow though, when we schedule an appointment in our calendar, we leave out key details. "Call with Rob" can remind us of our meeting, but when the time comes, we scan our email looking for the call-in number or the notes we needed to discuss.

Our calendars come equipped with loads of features. It can link to reference material, provide us with the correct call-in information, and several other options if we "tell it" that's what we need.

Forget what technology promises you it can do. Start with deciding what you want it to do. Then take the time to change the settings to deliver exactly what you need, when you need it. We all have preferences. The tools we already use can accommodate those preferences, if we just tell them what we need.

Success framing

In 2021 I hosted a show called *How I Use That!*, interviewed guests, mostly small business owners, asking them to show me some of the systems and software they used to run their businesses. I wasn't asking them for a software demonstration, as anyone can get that on YouTube. I was interested in the *unique* ways in which they chose to use the software.

- What do you do?
- How do you do it?
- What helps you do it?

To a person, each guest had established procedures to run their business. And no two did it the same way.

But the *real* magic came from *how* they use software to serve up exactly what they need when they need it.

One guest, Seth, used the term "extreme bookmarking" in his demonstration of how he used The Brain to not only keep track of information but also the relevant connections *between* information. For example, he had an entry for me that was connected to my friend, Chris Brogan, because that's how he came to know me. Paul's system had "deep links" behind each Trello card to ensure that everything he needs is simply a click away.

Tina and Kerry also had layers of relevant assets and notes for each project or card associated with the apps they showcased. Regardless of the application each person used, it was their established systems that provided the backbone. The core components were already in place. The applications they use simply made them work better.

Build from your needs

You already have systems in place. You may not follow them perfectly each time, but they're there. We have tasks we need to complete each day, week, month, or year. And we manage to get them done, at least *most* of the time.

Sometimes these systems are in our heads, regular activities we do from memory. But how often have you missed a step or spent time looking for information that would have made the whole thing easier?

Often, when things go wrong, it's because I didn't do something I *already* know I need to do to make it go right. In my process of reflective practice for the workshop I presented, I did, in fact, identify a few of the missteps, the points that, in my *personal* critique of my performance, left me with the feeling that I had "missed the mark." Let's call them *failures*. I also identified several points that went *very* well. After all, I did receive some positive feedback. Let's call those *successes*.

Remember my friend Kate's phrase? It was, "prepared *and* practiced." We built a Success Frame for giving presentations based on her phrase. It was also the result of reflective practice and asking myself the question, "What does it look like when it goes well?" and using a simple framework for reflective practice like the one above.

- What do you do?
- How do you do it?
- What helps you do it?

Here's the Success Frame we built for feeling confident going into a presentation:

- **Prepare**: Gather your information and build everything you need.
- **Practice**: Rehearse, review, test, walk it through.
- **Polish**: Spend more time on the parts that need tightening.
- **Present**: Deliver the product or presentation to your audience.

In reflecting on my speech, everything that went well was a result of having followed this process, well mostly. I had presented this material before many times. I had prepared well and practiced... most of it.

The areas that felt a bit off were the result of having added a few new slides. I didn't *practice* or *polish* those parts enough. As such, I didn't "hit the mark." The "failures" didn't provide me with new information. No, instead they pointed out that, in my preparation, I didn't adhere to my established Success Frame. In this case, deconstructing my "success" also pointed to the parts that were well rehearsed. The failures underscored the need for my personal Success Frame and how important it is.

The natural next question might be, "What does it look like when I use my Success Frames... well... *successfully?*"

We all have tasks we perform on a *somewhat* regular basis. Whether that's daily, weekly, monthly, or annually, there are many recurring events in our professional and personal lives. For me, many of those routine tasks, while necessary, can become a bit tedious. *It's also why I'm not a fan of formulas.*

However, I know what success looks like *for me* whenever I must complete these tasks. For our purposes, I'll sum it up with one word: Preparation. Of course, it's more than that. I know things go well for me when I've decided ahead of time which task I'll be working on and when. I know things go well for me when I have *everything I need* to complete the task laid out in front of me. I know things go well for me when I can make a task almost as easy as a habit, like tying my shoes.

Each component is summed up in my principle: Put success in your way.

Deciding ahead of time

If I have a regular task I perform, rather than try to remember each step, I create an ActionStack. These are simple, repeatable plans designed to help me stay focused.

Essentially, it's a step-by-step checklist based on what I know needs to be done to complete a task successfully. It's there to help me move through each step of a recurring process smoothly, without having to make a lot of in-the-moment decisions.

When I'm about to begin a recurring task, if I don't already have an ActionStack, I create one. I start by listing each step in the process and save it in Google Keep. That tool works for me. Yours may be something else.

The next time I need to complete the recurring task, I pull up my ActionStack and follow the steps. This simple system helps me to complete the task successfully with less effort. It has truly saved me hours of frustration.

For many of my ActionStacks, going through the steps works fine. For others, a bit of depth could serve me better. For example, there are several steps for setting up one of our webinars. I also use three or more separate software applications to put it all in place and get everyone registered.

What makes my ActionStack for hosting webinars more effective is having the links to each application embedded in each item on the checklist. Rather than reading through each step and going to my browser to get the link to Zoom or some other software, I added depth. This way, *everything I need* is already there. The supporting documents, information, and the links to each application are right where I need them. In doing this, I can make a task almost as easy as tying my shoes.

Building your Success Frame starts by looking at what you do and what it looks like when things go well. We need to ask ourselves the questions, "What does it look like when things go well?" and "What do I need?" If we do this, not *just* for the task as a whole but for each step, we can build Success Frames for almost anything we need to accomplish.

For me, my principle of preparation, "put success in your way," frames up my approach. Get specific about each step. Think about what you need, the links you use, the information that would be helpful to have close at hand. The software is not the system, but you can use it to make your system work for you.

What do *they* need—building frames for others

When you open the first door at Chipotle, the structure of the environment makes it very clear where the line is formed. You immediately and intuitively know how you're supposed to proceed to complete the process and end up with your food.

This is their customer Success Frame. Behind the scenes (or not, because Chipotle has an open kitchen environment) are all manner of operational Success Frames. There's a process in place used to order our food, all of which provides structure while also allowing for a certain amount of individualization. It ensures that the customer Success Frame functions as it should and (more often than not) generates the results that makes them successful.

I've done my fair share of email marketing. One of my favorite tips gets overlooked too often. It has nothing to do with the software we use, or how it works. It has nothing to do with which social platform you should use for marketing your business. One of the most important steps is to grab a piece of paper and a pen and begin to...

Map it out

More specifically, *map out the experience you want for your customer.*

If you have the good fortune to have someone arrive at your website, what is it that you want them to see? And perhaps more importantly, what's the most important thing for them to do?

- Are you hoping they'll sign up for your newsletter?
- Do you want them to schedule a call with you?
- Do you want them to buy your product or service?

More to the point, what do you *think* should happen next?

With every action someone takes, there should be a result. In the case of signing up for a newsletter, that may start with a "Thank you" page. And then the delivery of a welcome email.

The technology aspect of this is far less important than taking some time to map out each step. Consider the experience you want people to have. What do they need to have a successful experience?

If you were an architect designing a new hotel, you would consider everything, from what it's like when the doors open, to where you place the front desk. If you oversaw customer experience, you would want people to be friendly and warm and helpful.

So, after each step in the process, what happens next? The good news is that you get to decide what this looks like. It all starts with a sketch.

Here's a sample of the Success Frame my business partner, Chris Brogan, and I used when promoting a webinar:

- **Email One**: Seven days prior to event. Long form sales email. Link for direct purchase.
- **Email Two**: Five days prior. Rob's newsletter. Link to sales page.
- **Email Three**: Two days prior. Chris's newsletter. Link to sales page.

- **Email Four**: Day of webinar. Midmorning—helpful content. Link to sales page.
- **Email Five**: Day of webinar. Two hours prior—last call with brief summary. Link to sales page.

There are certain steps and rules for each email that need to be followed. Those are supported by ActionStacks.

ActionStacks are different to a Success Frame. ActionStacks are simple, repeatable plans designed to help you stay focused in the moment. They're a system to help move through each step of a recurring process quickly, without a whole lot of "decisions."

You can create ActionStacks for virtually any aspect of your life or business, from invoicing to customer service scenarios, from writing a blog post to parts of selling a webinar, from your exercise routine to weekly meal planning.

ActionStacks eliminate decisions, and help you move through the more routine parts of your day with greater effectiveness, efficiency, and ease, freeing up your brain for more important, creative, and meaningful activities. They're designed for use in a specific moment, and the completion of a specific operation in a series.

Success Frames, on the other hand, take a broader view. They could be a series of ActionStacks, an order of operations strung together that put you in the best position for a successful outcome.

To learn more about ActionStacks and how I use them, visit robhatch.com/actionstacks.

PART III

YOUR SUCCESS FRAMES

CHAPTER 7

SUCCESS FRAMES FOR AN AGE OF DISTRACTION

The topic of how addictive social media is, its impact, and its ability to essentially hack our brains has been covered extensively. What we're up against is so pervasive and powerful it has spawned everything from new economies to new psychological treatments.

In his book, *The Chaos Machine*, Max Fisher underscores one of the inherent challenges associated with managing not only our time and attention, in this age of distraction, but specifically how social media is primed to inflame your emotions.

So, let's set the stage of what we're up against.

> "Remember that the number of seconds in your day never changes. The amount of social media content competing for those seconds, however, doubles every year or so, depending on how you measure it. Imagine, for instance, that your network produces 200 posts a day, of which you have time to read about a hundred. Because of the platform's tilt, you will see the most outraged half of your feed. Next year, when 200 doubles to 400, you will see the most outraged

quarter, the year after that the most outraged eighth. Over time, your impression of your own community becomes radically more moralizing, aggrandizing and outraged. And so do you. At the same time, less innately engaging forms of content – truth, appeals to the greater good, appeals to tolerance – become more and more outmatched like stars over Times Square." – *The Chaos Machine*

Regardless of which slice of the political spectrum you occupy, these platforms aren't designed to serve you the *best* information or the most *balanced* perspective to help you arrive at a conclusion. Their goal, first and foremost, is to hook your interest and sustain your attention. And they do it very well.

This is what we're up against. And frankly, we weren't prepared for its power. Our attention has been hijacked, and we need tools that work *for* us to reclaim our attention and time.

One of us

Our addiction to our screens has become such a widely accepted problem that even mobile phone carriers are now talking about it. What's more, they're leveraging this problem, our frustration with our reliance on our devices, to sell us the devices that cause the problem.

In early 2023, a mobile carrier in the US (UScellular) launched a campaign called "Phones Down for 5." They've begun to promote the idea that we do, indeed, need time away from our phones. Of course, they're not wrong. It's a widely shared pain point and has been discussed and studied and written about.

The commercial features a brief scene where the CEO of UScellular articulates his concern about the issue and his commitment to addressing it. In another video, he specifically mentions that he's "doing something you may not expect" and encouraging us to put down our phones. UScellular even launched a page with a timer that defaults to five minutes, five hours, or five days along with the ability to set a custom timer. This is all part of their broader, "Let's find US again," campaign.

While I'm not sure how effective the campaign will be, positioning themselves as a company, correction, THE company that cares about this issue is an interesting approach. They're encouraging you to spend time doing *what* you love or being with who you love.

The cynic in me thinks, "Wow, they're so confident in the knowledge people are addicted to their devices that actively discouraging people from using them will not only have zero impact to the company's bottom line, it may actually increase it." After all, that's why companies spend money on marketing, to gain a bigger share of the market.

The closest thing I can think of here in the United States is when companies who sell alcohol promote moderation or encourage someone to be a designated driver, but I'm not sure whether that's more of a defensive legal strategy or court ordered or something along those lines. In that case, I would also imagine the hit is minimal and wonder about whether it would create an increase in revenue through brand loyalty or choice.

However, in the UScellular example, it feels pretty clear that they're communicating a message of caring so much that they're discouraging you from using the devices they actually sell, all with the goal of enticing your business.

And while they're appealing to this pain point to sell more devices, their approach, along with their confidence, underscores the pervasiveness of the problem.

Self-management in an age of distraction

In 2012, I began to notice the negative effects of various interruptions on my ability to complete my work. My ability to navigate the external demands on my time was becoming more and more difficult. And while I had, at that time, been recently diagnosed with ADHD and took medication for it, I didn't yet understand the role of ADHD in my life, the nature of it, and how the symptoms played out in my life each day.

If you're unfamiliar, ADHD is a neurological condition affecting at least one in 10 individuals. I say "at least" because there has been an increase in late/adult diagnoses in the past few years. So, it will be interesting to see future studies on its prevalence.

I sought a diagnosis for myself after pursuing one for my eldest son when he was 10 years old. His experiences and struggles in school bore an uncanny resemblance to my own at the same age. It became abundantly clear that I too should pursue a diagnosis and treatment.

It's not uncommon for adults diagnosed with ADHD to have developed some very successful coping mechanisms over the years. These coping mechanisms, along with a limited and incredibly skewed understanding of the challenges people with ADHD face, can effectively mask the diagnosis their entire life.

Many people with ADHD share similar stories of their school-age experience, having received reports from teachers with comments such as: "Robbie is a very bright boy. However, he talks too much with his friends and doesn't apply himself."

Even with a diagnosis, my understanding of the impact was heavily influenced by the prevailing understanding of the time about what ADHD looked like. Think "the overactive boy who talks too much in class and can't focus for a second." Some of that wasn't far off from my experience. I was the overactive, talkative boy. And as an adult I had simply found more acceptable outlets for that energy.

I had one other conversation that led me to pursue a diagnosis. I was talking with my friend, Paul, who was a few years older and a few years ahead of me in the parenting department. At the time, his son had also been recently diagnosed with ADHD. And, like me, the closer Paul looked, the more he identified with the struggles his young son was experiencing.

Paul was the valedictorian of his class and went on to an Ivy-League university, where the workload was intense to say the least. In classes, Paul was fine. He was engaged. He understood the material quite well. However, when he returned to his dorm to study, he struggled. His friends would sit and study for hours at a time, working through their assignments. Paul, on the other hand, struggled. Not because he wasn't as smart as his peers, but because he struggled to remain focused.

It's worth noting that this was in the late 1980s and early 1990s. The distraction of technology as we know it was still nearly two decades away.

He described what he experienced like this:

> "I knew I was just as capable as my classmates, but I would start working and then a thought or idea would distract me. I would look off at nothing, lost in thought until eventually, I'd catch myself. So, I would try to force myself to refocus, telling myself, 'Okay, you've got to focus. Get back to work.'

> "It worked for a short time but, inevitably, it would happen again 10 or 15 minutes later. I ended up going through this continuous loop of *focus, get distracted by a thought, stare off for a bit, catch myself, talk myself back, and then refocus for a bit*."

He also shared that as he entered his professional life he struggled with the same challenges at work.

As you might imagine, not knowing he had ADHD, the self-talk that happens when you try to refocus becomes decidedly more and more negative. And, as you can also guess, having to go through that thought loop over and over throughout the day, in addition to the energy required to do the actual work, is *exhausting*.

I identified with his story immediately. That loop sounded all too familiar.

In my conversation with Dr. Jayne Singer, she spoke of the impact of ADHD beyond the behavioral challenges it presents:

> "We have variations in temperament. We have variations in neurodevelopmental status and ADHD really does undermine a person's sense of self-agency because they feel so much at the whim of their impulses or distractions.
>
> "The more experiences that interfere with the development of that sense of independent mastery and control can truly lead to a sense of what Martin Seligman called 'Learned Helplessness.' That no matter what it is that I do, it doesn't work."

While I had developed a keen ability to mask my symptoms and "show up" in social and professional scenarios successfully for many years, I was also beginning to understand there was a tax I paid to do that. In addition to the exhaustion, I would often berate myself for not being able to focus.

This is just *one* example of the challenges people with ADHD experience, not only on a daily basis, but effectively all day long.

Unfortunately, at the time, I believed medication would be the fix. Well, that and a heavy dose of willpower. Medication can be very effective, and I'm supportive of people choosing to use it. However, I needed some additional adjustments, especially as social media emerged on to the scene and our devices found their way into our lives.

Oh, and relying on willpower never works by the way. That too gets taxed. But we'll get to that soon enough.

Aren't we all a bit ADHD?

No.

There's a growing sentiment outside the ADHD community that "everyone is a little ADHD." Not unlike my own misperceptions of ADHD, statements such as these are also misinformed. They fail to acknowledge the very real challenges people with ADHD struggle with daily. Sometimes simply to function.

Statements such as these are also quite harmful because they perpetuate the idea that it's simply a matter of learning to focus or trying harder. However, like Max Fisher alludes to in his book, our brains are, in many ways, being hacked by social media platforms. They're desperate for our attention, and while it may not be some nefarious plot, it's an algorithm after all, one that's programed to capture and maintain our attention.

So, when you feel compelled to check your phone endlessly throughout the day, or when you struggle to stop scrolling and return to the work at hand, it sometimes mimics what we "think" ADHD is. These culturally induced attention behaviors have permeated our daily lives as a set of habits that, in some ways, mimic many of the commonly associated symptoms of ADHD, particularly inattentive-type symptoms.

And again, it's worth noting that the commonly associated symptoms are still based on a grossly misinformed and misunderstood idea of what ADHD looks like. Of course, these culturally induced behaviors can be challenging for anyone. However, for someone with ADHD the stakes are even higher. This makes finding ways to successfully manage distractions more important than ever.

While the stakes have changed, *before* the prevalence of social media distractions came in a few simple forms, at least for me:

- People were distracting
- Thoughts were distracting

People–managing boundaries

The ways in which a person could interrupt were limited. To gain our attention they had to enter our physical or audible space in person or via a phone call. Before social media fully burst on to the scene, even email was very much viewed as a business communication tool and, as such, was constrained by the narrow scope of what was acceptable in business. It hadn't fully infiltrated our consciousness. Add to that, there were detractors for electronic communication in the early days and their voices were still quite loud.

So, distractions were still somewhat limited.

As a young leader rising through the ranks in the early 1990s through the early 2000s, I had adopted the false notion of the "open-door manager." The idea was that leaders should always be available and accessible. I say "false" notion because it's not a sustainable approach. And despite the wonderful intentions of being available to the people one supervises, it didn't allow for the focused time necessary to do the work required of the position.

Regardless, my young, nimble mind, still unaware of its ADHD, seemed to navigate those interruptions with ease. People would come into my office and I believed I could make the switch easily to attending to their needs.

Looking back, it was as though I craved the switch. Each interruption provided the very welcome hit of dopamine my brain craved. It kept me engaged. People rarely entered my office to tell me things were perfect. They came to me to work through a challenge, to seek my counsel and opinion.

Here's what was actually happening. On any given day, I might be working on a project that required my focus and attention, such as writing a grant application. One of my staff would come to my door and ask whether I had a minute. Operating from the notion that I should remain accessible, I would agree, welcome them in, and they would sit in a chair across the desk from me. Meanwhile, the grant I was working on would remain open on my computer, which was sitting to the side of my desk, and while not directly between us, was still within my line of sight.

For the first few moments of the conversation, and sometimes beyond, my attention was split. I was still thinking about the grant, while also trying to give the person in front of me the attention they deserved. Remember Sophie Leroy's study? She called this "attention residue." Each time we switch from one thing to the next, we carry with us cognitive remnants of the last task.

But that wasn't the worst part of it. I began to feel frustrated and resentful of the interruption. After all, I was trying to work on a grant application, the money for which not only enabled us to fund programs but also paid our salaries. Don't they know how important this work is? Of course not.

When I finally acknowledged the frustration I was experiencing, I realized that my "open-door policy" needed some adjusting. It may have created the *impression* of being available and supportive. However,

I didn't like the fact that my attention was split between two very important needs. In the end, no one was getting the attention they deserved.

I needed to find a way to be more effective at maintaining boundaries but still be available. It was *very important* to me that the people I served in this organization knew that I valued their needs as well. The solution had to also communicate this.

Everyone wants to be heard

What does that look like? The point of having an open-door policy was to be available for employees to hear their ideas and their concerns. So, I made a simple but important change and started a subtle shift in the way I communicated in those moments.

As people came to my door to ask for a few minutes of my time, I began to share my intentions openly, especially if I was already working on a project. It looked something like this: "I'm sorry, but I'm working on this <project> right now, but I really want to hear what you have to say. I can meet with you in X minutes. I just need to wrap this up first so I can give you my full attention."

Sometimes it was 30 minutes or we would schedule a time later in the day. But it became a simple, effective framework for remaining available, while also setting boundaries. And by owning the fact that if I were to stop I wouldn't be giving them my full attention, I was communicating how much I value our relationship. And how important it was for me to be present for them.

As we discussed in the first chapter, the failure of my "open-door policy" pointed out the problem but it didn't teach me how to solve the problem. Much like the space between stimulus and response, the feeling of frustration caused me to pause.

Finding the solution came from asking myself some questions:

- What do I want these interactions to look like?
- What does it look like when I'm fully present?
- What do I need to do to be at my best for my employees?

And the solution came from anchoring myself in the principle of *valuing the relationship*.

Thoughts—managing my attention

My brain can be a bit of a jerk. It interrupts me when I'm trying to focus, mostly with little things that could easily wait. But my brain is also quite clever. It disguises these interruptions and recasts them as "helpful reminders."

- Don't forget to call your mother.
- Remember to schedule the kids' dentist appointments.
- Did you reply to that email?

Helpful, right? Not necessarily. When those thoughts come into my head, the tendency is to stop what I'm doing. I want to take care of it immediately because "it will only take a minute" and "if I don't do it right now, I'll probably forget."

But those tasks are never that urgent. They can wait. Switching is disruptive and takes me away from my work.

We also know it rarely ends there. As soon as I shift my focus to make a quick call or shoot off a short email, something else grabs my attention and on and on.

Thought capturing

Two of the most essential tools I use for managing distractions are a pen and a blank sheet of paper. I start each day with a new page. Whenever my brain gives me a "helpful reminder," I just write it down and return to my work. It's that simple.

This way, the reminder is safely captured, and my mind is at ease, knowing I won't forget. I always make time later in my day to review the list and take care of each item.

This has been especially useful when working from home and the dynamics of work have changed. The lines between life at home and work have blurred even more, and my brain is sending me helpful reminders at a furious pace. My blank page helps with that.

Establish rules

I had a few "unexpected interruptions" in my day recently. At least that's what we'll call them for the moment. It happens. I'm sure it happens to you as well. The nature of the unexpected isn't all that important. Suffice it to say, they took me away from my work and took a bit more time than I would have liked.

But instead of lamenting my day going sideways and all I didn't accomplish, I'm taking a second look, to take stock of what *really* happened.

I had decided the night before what I was going to work on, specifically what would define success for that day. So, I started the day knowing exactly what to do and had everything I needed for my three most important projects.

I followed my rules for how I approach that block of time. I didn't check social media, email, and didn't answer calls. Because of this, I was able to focus and accomplish a great deal of my planned work before the *unexpected* happened. And that's a better phrase, that the unexpected *happened*.

Earlier, I called it an unexpected *interruption*. And while that's technically true, let's look at the slow-motion replay. Perhaps we'll reconsider what an interruption is and what's something that happens, allowing us to make a conscious shift of our attention.

So, let's start at the point where I'm blissfully working on my project. All is going well right up to the point when I get the *second* notification from my wife. This our bat signal. The second call is a trigger. It means, "Hey, I know you're working, but there's this *other* thing that's more important than what you're doing." Typically, this is a family matter, and because this rule is well established, I don't even have to think about it. This isn't an interruption; it's a predetermined rule anchored to an established priority, my family.

At that moment and because we have that rule in place, I deliberately shifted my attention from what I *had* been working on to what I *knew* mattered more without even needing to know what it was. It's all right there on the replay.

And, on the *one* hand, this was "unexpected." It did, by definition, interrupt the work I had been doing. On the *other* hand, my wife and I planned for this scenario. We *decided ahead of time* that our family gets top priority when it comes to where we choose to focus our attention.

I share this with you because I didn't understand this in the moment. I needed the replay to see it for what it was. I share this with you because we sometimes think focus and attention are all about increased productivity and achieving more. I share this with you, not because the day went the way I planned. I definitely didn't get everything done that I set out to do. But, in the end, because I had an established framework for making decisions in these situations, I *did* choose to focus my time and attention on what matters.

In my final assessment of the day, what I failed to get done is vastly outweighed by the fact that, even though it wasn't what I set out to accomplish, everything went according to plan.

Operate from Your priorities

One of the most effective ways for directing our attention and managing the deluge of information and distractions is to operate from our priorities. Our priorities emerge from our values.

Of course, we all value different things. However, one of the more common values people share with me during training and when I work with them one on one is their relationships with the people they love, whether they're family or friends.

Our relationships with people we love, how we nurture and foster those connections can be one of our best sources for ideas and inspiration for building a framework that helps us make the best decisions for how we spend our time and energy.

CHAPTER 8

BUILDING YOUR FRAMES

My friend Matthew lives on 58 acres in rural Maine. He has never been interested in simply owning a home on a small plot of land in a neighborhood. It's been his dream to live on a plot of land large enough to create an experience, or even a set of experiences. Over the years, Matthew has shaped his property to provide him and anyone who visits with a variety of environments to suit different moods or experience nature in different seasons. And it all began by exploring.

Matthew walked the old paths through the woods, discovering the unique features of his property. He found an old stone wall, a vernal stream, an old logging road, and a small, overgrown apple orchard nearly choked by vines. With each walk, Matthew would clean a bit more of the path or cut away some of the overgrowth. He felled trees to create the perfect spots to sit and enjoy a sunset in June. Recently, he cleared decades of sediment from a massive ledge on the highest point in his woods.

What started as a small, four-foot square patch of exposed ledge is now a few hundred square feet of smooth rock. It's the perfect place to lie back on a hot summer night and feel the coolness of the granite as you stare up at the stars.

Every nook and cranny provides opportunity for experience. Matthew sees this and then methodically shapes the land to create the experience he wants for himself and the people who visit him.

You and I may not have acres of land to play with, but we enter a series of environments from the moment we open our eyes each morning. Each environment influences how we experience our day. It's true of our homes, offices, and our devices. These are the spaces in which we spend our time.

The nature of each environment may be different. But it's important to remember that we get to shape the landscape and create the experiences we want from the moment we open our eyes.

What works for you?

If you could design exactly how you want to wake up each day and what you would like to have available and ready, what would that look like? How would you frame it?

When you arrive at work, what do you need to be successful at your job? *My* first inclination is to look for a way to make certain things a little easier. I'm not afraid of hard work; I just want the hard work to be as efficient and effective as possible. So, I tend to scan for friction points and either eliminate them or adjust the environment to reduce the level of resistance.

In my book *Attention!* I talk extensively about a core principle I call "put success in your way." You can learn more about it at robhatch.com/psiyw. Essentially, it's rooted in three core elements:

- Willpower is limited
- Decisions are distractions
- Habits are a powerful force

When shaping any environment and creating the experience I want to have, I ask myself three questions:

- How can I decrease my reliance on willpower?
- How can I remove decisions?
- How can I make this as automatic as a habit?

My goal is to find ways to make an experience easier or, as in the case of Matthew, more enjoyable.

The space to ask

A weird controversy bubbled up in early 2023. Famed expert on keeping things tidy, Marie Kondo, shared that she's now embracing "messiness." As a mother of three young children, Kondo is no longer tidying her home daily. Instead, she's enjoying time with her family and worrying less about the state of her house.

The reactions to Kondo's confession have run the gamut from deep sighs of relief to feelings of outright betrayal.

Let's be clear. I'm sure Marie Kondo isn't suddenly living like a hoarder. Her version of "messy" probably looks a lot tidier than mine. However, to borrow her famous phrase, her family is what "sparks joy" for her now.

I must confess that I adopted some of Kondo's techniques, specifically her method for folding clothes and organizing my dresser. But the gem in Kondo's process isn't learning how to fold your T-shirts into neat little envelopes. Instead, the *real* magic resides in her simple question, "Does this spark joy?" More specifically, pausing to *ask* that question.

Stopping in the busyness of our lives, even for a moment, to check in and ask ourselves a simple question can be powerful. Especially when that question asks is this what I want? In many ways, this is the space between stimulus and response that Viktor Frankl is encouraging us to find.

Kondo's question shares the same core aim—to slow things down, restore our locus of control, and making choices with purpose and intention.

When Kondo initially posed the question, "Does this spark joy?", her purpose was to help us declutter our lives. She encouraged us to confront the "stuff" we surround ourselves with in our homes and ask, "Does this (lamp, painting, shirt, empty shoe box) bring me joy?"

Some of Marie Kondo's followers and disciples were confused and disappointed by her comments on embracing messiness. It felt like a betrayal and a deviation from her teaching a lifestyle of tidiness. But it doesn't feel like a betrayal to me.

While she has taught many specific techniques on the "art of decluttering and organizing," the core of her approach was always pausing to ask, "Does this spark joy?"

As a mother, her priorities have shifted. The experience she wants to create for herself and her children is different. So, no. She hasn't abandoned her teachings; she's still asking the same question, only she's broadened it to include her children and how she spends her time with them. Perhaps it sounds something like, "Which gives me *more* joy: Time with my children, or tidying my home?"

What do I want... to eat?

Cheryl K. Johnson is a wellbeing strategist and author of the book *Box Lunch Lifestyle*. Johnson takes a similar approach to creating the space to pause and consider our power to make choices. She does this by using the shared experience of eating lunch.

In an interview, Johnson shared how asking the simple question "what do *I* want to eat?" can effectively make the somewhat abstract notion of *mindfulness* more concrete.[19]

Of course, there are some rules to her box lunch lifestyle approach. I'm guessing they help ensure we don't eat twinkies every day. But by applying this question to part of our day that, however small, *belongs* to us,

---

[19] https://kristenmanieri.com/episode185/

she's giving us a tool to expand our *locus of control*. Johnson reminds us that we can pause and check in with ourselves.

Much like Marie Kondo's encouragement to ask ourselves "does this spark joy?" it's easy to see how Johnson's simple question of "what do I want to eat?" can expand to *other* areas. Both can cultivate a practice of pausing to ask, "What do I want to spend my time doing?" and can become, as Cheryl K. Johnson notes, an entire "lifestyle."

Leaning into success—the 43%

As it turns out, approximately 43% of those who set new year's resolutions end up quitting before the end of January. It's easy to focus our attention on why these people *failed* to make it past four weeks of what was to be a year-long journey. Maybe it's even happened to you.

And, if you're anything like me, it's also easy to imagine the self-defeating thoughts that inevitably enter our minds when this happens: "See, there you go again, you can't follow through." "You're never consistent." "You *always* do this. You say you're going to xxx and then..." You get the picture.

And sure, we could hone in on all the reasons we failed. But, as Fishbach's study alludes, our egos take a bit of a hit. And if you don't believe the study, how closely did you identify with the negative self-talk?

If it's true that our egos make it more difficult for us to learn from failure, why are we spending time fighting that to potentially extract a lesson from our failure, especially when our ego is essentially lying to us by saying, "You failed because you're a piece of shit."

Focus on strengths

I've mentioned my mentor, Dr. T. Berry Brazelton, before. His Touchpoints Approach to working with children and families has had a profound impact on the world of child development. It has also changed how practitioners approach their work with children and families.

Dr. Brazelton developed a list of principles and assumptions for working with families. The assumptions serve to guide our thinking and help us approach an interaction with the right mindset.

One of those assumptions is "all parents have strengths." That one phrase can shift our mindset, our view of the situation, and, most importantly, our view of the person. This is especially helpful when, by all appearances, it seems like everything is falling apart. It serves as a powerful reminder to look beyond the situation. It helps us resist the urge to focus on a person's deficits, the desire to try to fix, and instead look for strengths.

And why is this important? Because everyone has strengths. And strengths give us something upon which to build.

Of course, you know I'm not just talking about working with parents. This is also about how we see ourselves. This is about how we focus on the mistakes we've made, the times we've failed, the "there I go again" moments. It's about thinking we need to fix what's wrong rather than building on what's right.

Instead of looking at the point of failure for our resolutions, what if we reframe our approach to examine the success we experienced in the first four weeks of the year?

Let's say your resolution was to go to the gym every day. For the first 22 days you nailed it. You were already starting to notice a difference in how you feel. You lost 7lbs. You're eating better, hydrating more, everything is clicking. In the last week though, you fell off your daily pace. You missed two days in a row, went back one day, but you haven't been in four days straight.

I don't want to know why you failed. I want to know how you managed to go to the gym every day for 22 days. I want to know what motivated you to set the resolution in the first place. I want to know how, despite all your commitments to work, time with family, and all the other demands and temptations, you were able to get to the gym and remained consistent for that long?

What did that look like?

My coaching clients hear this question often. It's what I ask when I want them to go beyond talking about an idea or an event to share greater detail. It's a useful tool for beginning to identify the elements that contributed to a successful run.

Rather than focus on what went wrong on day 23, I believe we can learn much more from how you managed to go to the gym each day for over three weeks straight. Any time you can string together a series of consistent actions, you're building a method for personal success, even if you don't make it all the way.

In each accomplishment there's a series of actions. There were steps you took to make it happen. What did that look like?

- What did you do?
- What did you set up for yourself to make it work?

And then what did you do?

First, look at all the control those questions are asking you to tell. "You do" and "you set up." That's ownership. Yes, we get to own our successes as well.

So maybe your answers are something like this:

- I woke up a half-hour early.
- I put it on my calendar.
- I had my workout clothes packed.
- I had coffee ready.
- I had a plan for exactly what I would be doing when I got there.

Any list you make will likely contain vital clues and patterns for the actions that produced your result. At the very least they're a simple process for restarting whatever you might have finished. At their best, they're a map you can use for other goals.

- Decide ahead of time what I'm doing
- Schedule it
- Have what I need ready

Can you see how that starts to turn into a framework for success? It's not everything. It's not failproof. But the more you do it, the longer you string the actions together, the more you'll have to build on.

For me, setting up my day the night before with the three most important things that I need to accomplish, written out, helps support my experience as I enter my day. Having a blank piece of paper next to me is a place to easily capture the ideas that enter my mind, without interrupting my workflow while ensuring I don't forget the idea.

We must ask (and answer) the question "what would that look like?" with regards to the various points in our day.

What does it look like when things go well?

At first glance, we get it. We nod our head and, on premise, agree with the idea of taking back control. But if we don't reflect on this question regularly, we miss the point.

Maybe something isn't working for you at home or at your job. The reasons may be long or short, but probably involves some form of prioritization, procrastination, organization, or distraction. Interestingly, this list of reasons why it's not working always seems to come more easily to us. Rarely, if ever, can we list the reasons why something worked for us.

It's important to reflect on your success to identify a successful process. The point of the exercise isn't some warm and fuzzy "don't forget that you're special and great" rah-rah. It's rooted in the idea that we so often ignore—the fact that we've built our own frameworks for success. And they're frameworks we can replicate, adjust, and build upon to take on new challenges in the future.

Success Frames aren't meant to be a specific formula we follow, but a framework rooted in our individual experience, supporting us to achieve new goals.

CHAPTER 9

OUR FRAMES SUPPORT OUR ACTIONS

We can construct a repeatable framework for success, one that we can adapt to help support us in new circumstances, to accomplish new goals. But they don't do the work *for* us.

Ultimately, we want our Success Frames to support us to take the actions necessary to achieve success. That requires defining success. We can do that by asking, "What does success look like?"

Defining success

As my wife was calculating her sales tax at the end of the quarter, she mentioned that her revenue was up almost 21% compared to the same period the year prior. I thought that sounded like a pretty impressive number.

Interestingly, revenue isn't her definition of a successful quarter. The way she sees it, revenue is the result of a successful quarter. And the distinction is important.

What drives the results? Meg specializes in portrait photography. She has two main client categories: High school seniors and families. She also knows what her average revenue is per client for each category. However, when she's establishing goals for her business, she doesn't focus on revenue, she focuses on the client.

Specifically, her focus is to increase the number of clients who book a session with her. And while this may seem simple and perhaps even obvious, the shift from revenue goals to client goals is an important distinction. She understands that when she focuses her attention on serving people, the results will come. And this shift from establishing a revenue goal to increasing the number of clients who choose to book, frames her approach to everything she does.

Megin spends her time creating experiences for her clients. She doesn't just post pictures on her marketing channels; she tells stories that draw people closer. She encourages moms (and dads and grandparents) to "get in the picture," candidly sharing how she wishes she had shed her insecurities years ago.

She takes time to connect with all the relatives and friends who comment on the sneak peek portrait of the high school graduate she just shared. You know, the one where the teenager is laughing in a way that perhaps he or she hadn't in a while. And it's the people who know this teenager best who recognize how perfectly she captured their unique personality.

Her focus on the client pushes her to ask, "How can I get more people in the picture?" It's a great goal to strive to achieve. And if she succeeds, she knows the results will speak for themselves.

How you define success matters. It helps us ensure that our frame is built to support the actions required to achieve success. By Megin's definition, she's hoping to *create the context in which she can do her best work.*

I mentioned in Chapter 8 that one of my personal Success Frames is "put success in your way." In fact, I use it to help me build other Success Frames. Here's a reminder of the three elements:

- Willpower is a limited resource
- Decisions are distractions
- Habits are a powerful force

While we have the capacity to call upon and exert willpower toward accomplishing a goal, studies have shown that willpower isn't an inexhaustible resource, particularly throughout the course of the day. With that in mind, we don't want to *rely* on whatever stores of willpower we have to do anything we might categorize as a mundane task.

The example I like to use is, if my goal is to train for a 10k, I don't want to use my willpower to get myself out of bed and out the door. I would rather utilize it *during* the run when things get tough.

So, it makes sense to consider how to apply our efforts effectively and efficiently. It makes sense to direct it toward areas of your life that matter the most.

Much like willpower, our decision-making abilities also become taxed throughout the day. For every decision we make, our ability to make subsequent decisions decreases. I don't want to start my day walking through my house looking for car keys, thinking about what I want to have for breakfast or what to wear. Each one of those actions requires a decision, however small. Each decision takes a moment of our time, however short. And every small decision requires energy I would rather put toward something else.

Habits are a powerful force to which we're biologically prone. This is not to say we're completely governed by our habits. However, we're biologically prone to form them and they play a valuable function in getting us through our day. It's because of our habits that we don't have to expend mental energy thinking about things such as *how* we brush our teeth or the process of tying our shoes. They're ingrained habits. Habits make things easier. They unburden our minds and allow us to move through the day more efficiently. I want to use this biological tendency to my advantage.

"Put success in your way" accepts these three core elements and leverages our understanding of them to make things easier. Let's look closer at how we can utilize this as a Success Frame.

I developed one of my cornerstone Success Frames through reflective practice, supported by my friend and coach, Becky McCray. As I've mentioned, as someone with ADHD I can become distracted easily. Some of the other challenges I experience are procrastination and managing interruptions (internal and external). But I've also experienced times when I've successfully managed *all* those challenges.

I can recount a time when I experienced taking time away from my usual confines. So as not to interrupt time with my family while on vacation, I decided to get up early each morning to put in a bit of work on a few projects. Becky and I deconstructed my success. The result was a framework that has continued to support me to maintain my focus and improve my personal productivity. I call this framework my "success block."

The key for me is to approach the first two hours of each day in the same way I did when I experienced this success. It looks like this:

1. Planned: I decide which projects I'll work on *ahead of time*. Usually the night before.
2. Project-limited: I limit my "success block" to three specific projects.
3. Time-limited: I schedule a specific amount of time (two hours).
4. Time-specific: I allow each project 45 minutes.
5. Free from interruption: I turn off all notifications. I don't check email or take phone calls.

Each step leverages one or more of the three components of "put success in your way." I shared a basic framework for this earlier:

- Decide ahead of time what I'm doing
- Schedule it
- Have what I need ready

I rely on those basic frameworks quite often. I talked before about finding ways to leverage success in one area to apply it to others.

State your intentions— a mini-frame

There's something wonderfully simple and powerful about setting our intentions and stating them out loud.

Sometimes our schedules are thrown off and we need to adjust and get back to work. For me, the challenge of restarting can be difficult. When this happens, I break things down into short time blocks and set my intention. "For the next 25 minutes I'll…" This is my quick version of *deciding ahead of time* and I also utilize other elements of my "success block" frame.

Stating our intention does a few things:

- *It slows us down.* There's a harried nature to our lives. I notice that even when I'm doing nothing my brain can be a wobbly mess of thoughts and competing urges to work on this or that. Combine that with the guilt of what I *should* be doing instead of nothing. Taking a moment to state my intention is a lot like finding the space Frankl talks about. It clears away what I *was* doing and sets me up for what I'm about to do.
- *I take ownership of my time.* When I state my intention of, say, writing for 25 minutes, I'm laying claim to that time for that purpose. Whatever is in my inbox doesn't matter during

that time. It doesn't matter what's happening on TikTok or CNN. That time is reserved.

- *It defines the action.* Stating my intention brings definition and focus to my actions. There's a clarity about what I'm doing with the next 25 minutes of my day. If I were entering a meeting, I might also take a quiet moment to myself to state my intention beforehand. Reminding myself of this focuses my attention on the people and the purpose.

What I find most effective about this approach is the simple reminder of what I'll be doing and the act of giving myself permission to focus on *one* thing. I keep the time increments short. I choose 25-minute or 45-minute time blocks. As I gain focus, I sometimes string a series of intentions and actions together.

To be clear, I don't always have everything decided and prepared. But this mini-frame leverages many of the same elements that I've come to rely on to replicate success.

Simple decisions—a mini-frame

Decisions being distractions is one element of "put success in your way" that I get reminded of time and time again.

In the first four months of the pandemic, there were so many activities I considered doing. As the weather warmed here in Maine, the temptation to get out and *do* something, *anything*, grew. But what?

Besides a few socially distant gatherings with a small group of friends or family, we hadn't left the house much. And safe and fun (for me) activities weren't in abundance. And then I would think... "I should take the canoe out on the river." "I should go fishing." "I should go golfing with my mom or my friend."

But my brain would clap back with... "Yeah, but the canoe is too heavy for one person. You haven't even looked at it in a year." "You don't have all the gear you need for fishing. Where would you even go?" "It will take too long."

As is often the case with a good idea, the space between where I sit and getting myself out the door is the most treacherous gap to navigate. My brain loves to point out all the work required, what I don't have, and what I need but can't get. It loves to put *when* and *how* and *what if* in front of me. These are the things in my way.

The power of simple decisions

One afternoon I *decided* to take 15 minutes and went to my garage to look over the canoe. Everything seemed fine, so I checked to make sure I also had the oars, life vests, and anchor.

The next day I took another 15 minutes and went through our fishing equipment. I gathered a few rods and some tackle and pulled it together.

That evening I decided to go through my fly-fishing gear, which I hadn't used in years. I sat in front of the television and for 30 minutes I reacquainted myself with everything. I cleaned a few things and got it ready.

A few days later there I was in our canoe on a local river watching my 10-year-old daughter reel in her first fish. Over the next two weeks I fished four times. I went with my son, spent an entire day with my brother, taught my daughter, and even managed a few hours fishing on my own.

The canoe is too heavy for one person. *I checked. It wasn't.*

You haven't even looked at it in a year. *I checked. It's fine.*

You don't have all the gear you need. *I looked. I did.*

Where would you even go? *I looked at a map. It was close.*

It will take too long, and you don't have the time. *It might. But I made time.*

I wish I could say I planned each step. *I didn't.* What I did was tackle the small stuff getting in the way, bit by bit. What I did is what has worked for me in the past whenever I've wanted to accomplish something. Even something as simple as going fishing. I removed the barriers by intentionally claiming small bits of time and focusing on one thing at a time. I removed all the tiny decisions keeping me from doing something I wanted.

Navigating the transitions

It was that time of year for me. It may not line up exactly the same for you, but each spring a reminder shows up in my calendar for the past few years: "Adjust—The end of the school year gets crazy."

And sure enough, my wife and I had already begun talking about navigating the impending transition to summer schedules. It's all normal. It happens every year in some form. And we always manage to find our way through it successfully. But it's a lot all at once. And the impact extends beyond our family life to our respective businesses. So, adjustments needed to be made on all fronts.

But the importance of that reminder can't be overstated. It serves as a healthy dose of anticipatory guidance before finding ourselves immersed in the chaos and questioning our sanity. Honestly, just knowing it's about to happen is reassuring and makes navigating the whole thing that much easier.

In late spring, our daughter is finishing the last few weeks of school, and her siblings are coming home from college for the summer. So, inevitably, I must adjust my current schedule. For example, I need to block off more time to attend end-of-year events, get everyone home, and settled in for the summer.

Having an annual reminder before it happens provides me with some anticipatory guidance. This allows me to prepare and adjust.

If you drive to work, you may have noticed message boards appearing on the side of the road a few weeks before construction. The idea is to inform you that the route you typically use and the amount of time it takes to get to your destination will be different for a few weeks. Ideally, this gives you time to prepare and adjust your schedule to leave more time for your commute.

The same is true with my annual reminders. I know from experience when my family will experience disruption from their regular routine. And those reminders are my personal message board.

Here are a few of the critical transition points in our family and when I set my reminders:

- End of the school year—six weeks prior
- Beginning of the school year—three to four weeks prior
- End of the year holidays (late November through the first week in January)—one to two weeks before Thanksgiving and again two weeks before Christmas

The adjustments don't have to be major to have a significant impact. A simple reminder of how busy things will be helps me reset my expectations for what I can accomplish during the transition.

These reminders, the anticipatory guidance, points me to the things that have supported me in the past, my Success Frames.

- Decide ahead of time what I'm doing
- Have what I need ready
- Schedule it

Truthfully, these notifications have saved me enormous amounts of frustration. Sometimes I just need a reminder that getting where I'm going may take a bit more time.

It's important to remember that our professional and personal lives have seasons. Sometimes this require us to make adjustments. So, if things aren't entirely working the way they were a month ago, it might be time to tweak your routines.

- Take notice of what's happening around you
- Look for opportunities to adjust
- Be deliberate
- Make notes about what works and when the changes came
- Build a simple frame to help make future season shifts that much more effective
- Create a reminder for the same time next year

And remember, this is happening to everyone.

A decision frame

I work with clients who face a range of important decisions about their businesses. Some due to recent dramatic growth and others who are considering the need to pivot in small or significant ways. The common denominator with both is uncertainty.

For those who are in demand, there are concerns about how long it will last and how much growth they can handle. The same is true of those looking to pivot. Should they shift temporarily, or will this be permanent?

Business owners have always had to contend with unexpected events. They've always faced difficult choices. Uncertainty creates a level of urgency that can turn into overwhelm and anxiety. All of this clouds our ability to see the actual problem.

Name it

Sometimes we *think* we know what we're struggling with because it feels like it's all you can think about. The truth is, we've probably lost sight of the real issue.

By naming the problem, or at least attempting to, it gives us something concrete. We *need* to get it out of our heads. Talking through an idea or writing it out can sometimes give us enough to work with.

What decisions are you facing in your business right now? Take a moment and write your answer. Don't take too long. Just write for a few minutes and see if you can't identify the issue more clearly. When you have that, try these two questions on for size:

- What's the first step you need to take?
- What do you need to know to help you make the decision confidently?

Start there. Keep it brief.

I've shared numerous Success Frames with you in this chapter and throughout the book. Many of them come from mining the lessons of my own success, large and small. I believe that many of them, like the frameworks emerging from "put success in your way," can be useful to many people in many situations.

However, the clarity that comes from identifying your personal strengths is truly powerful. Of course, there are assessment tools designed to categorize our strengths. And those tools can be very useful, giving us a common language to talk about our broader strengths.

But reflecting on our past success, understanding the choices we made, the actions we took and *how* we put it all together is a rich and untapped source of strength. Beyond that, our ability, as Traci Sponenberg noted, to "adapt to the needs of the person" is how we can discover the unique strengths of the people within our organizations.

One way to do this is to provide opportunities for reflective practice where people can "engage in a continuous cycle of self-observation and self-evaluation in order to understand their own actions" with the goal of observing and refining their skills and abilities.

Leaders themselves can support this, not only by providing those opportunities, but by engaging in reflective supervision aimed at supporting this process. And all with the goal of understanding each person's unique strengths and abilities and providing them with what they need to bring them to bear.

For additional resources on reflective practice and reflective supervision, visit robhatch.com/reflectivepractice

NEXT STEPS:
WHAT DOES THAT LOOK LIKE?

There it is again, my favorite question. Truth be told, I don't know what *your* next steps will be, but I do have some simple suggestions and things I would encourage you to try.

For you

Cultivate your own reflective practice. Start small. Set aside 20 minutes a week. Think about a situation, an interaction you had, a project you completed, or a recent accomplishment.

Ask yourself some version of the question, "What did success look like?" Allow yourself to tell the story of *how* you managed to achieve a successful outcome. If you enjoy writing, write it down. Alternatively, turn on the voice recorder app on your phone or shoot a video.

Focus on what you did, what you said, and the choices you made. And acknowledge the help you may have received. Maybe it was support from a friend, advice from a mentor, or accountability check-ins from a teammate or coach.

Make note of what worked for *you* and see if you can identify some core elements that you've relied on in the past. These will become part of your Success Frame.

For others

If you happen to be in a position of providing support to others, whether at work, with a significant other, or with your children. Practice looking for their strengths.

Ask them to tell you *their* stories of success. Ask them how they managed to do that. Ask them about the choices they made, what they did, or said. See if you can identify some of their core elements to help build their Success Frame.

And thank you for your time and attention. I appreciate it more than you know.

For additional material, and to learn more about Success Frames visit robhatch.com/successframes. Or drop me a line at rob@robhatch.com. Seriously. I would love to hear from you.

ABOUT THE AUTHOR

Rob Hatch is an author and sought-after coach for business owners and executives. He brings a unique blend of knowledge and background into the field of human development with his experience as a successful business leader and coach.

He has written a weekly newsletter for over a decade, read by tens of thousands of individuals worldwide.

As a coach, Rob works primarily with business leaders and teams, guiding them through critical organizational transitions.

He's the author of the international best-selling book *Attention! The Power of Simple Decisions in a Distracted World*, named a 2021 Business Book of the Year Finalist.

Rob lives in Maine with his award-winning photographer wife, Megin. They have four children and spend most of their time encouraging and supporting them as they pursue their passions.

INDEX

A quick word from Practical Inspiration Publishing...

We hope you found this book both practical and inspiring – that's what we aim for with every book we publish.

We publish titles on topics ranging from leadership, entrepreneurship, HR and marketing to self-development and wellbeing.

Find details of all our books at: www.practicalinspiration.com

 Did you know...

We can offer discounts on bulk sales of all our titles – ideal if you want to use them for training purposes, corporate giveaways or simply because you feel these ideas deserve to be shared with your network.

We can even produce bespoke versions of our books, for example with your organization's logo and/or a tailored foreword.

To discuss further, contact us on info@practicalinspiration.com.

 Got an idea for a business book?

We may be able to help. Find out more about publishing in partnership with us at: bit.ly/PIpublishing.

Follow us on social media...

@PIPTalking

@pip_talking

@practicalinspiration

@piptalking

Practical Inspiration Publishing

Printed in the USA
CPSIA information can be obtained
at www.ICGtesting.com
JSHW011416160824
R13664500003B/R136645PG68134JSX00030B/3